HOW TO
PROFIT IN THE
STOCK MARKET

HOW TO
PROFIT IN THE
STOCK MARKET

SHORT-TERM TRADING AND INVESTING
STRATEGIES FOR BEGINNERS

MICHAEL SINCERE

NEW YORK   CHICAGO   SAN FRANCISCO   ATHENS   LONDON
MADRID   MEXICO CITY   MILAN   NEW DELHI
SINGAPORE   SYDNEY   TORONTO

1 2 3 4 5 6 7 8 9   LCR   27 26 25 24 23 22

ISBN   978-1-264-26731-6
MHID   1-264-26731-2

e-ISBN   978-1-264-26732-3
e-MHID   1-264-26732-0

This publication is designed to provide accurate and authoritative information in regard to the subject matter covered. It is sold with the understanding that neither the author nor the publisher is engaged in rendering legal, accounting, securities trading, or other professional services. If legal advice or other expert assistance is required, the services of a competent professional person should be sought.
    —*From a Declaration of Principles Jointly Adopted by a Committee of the American Bar Association and a Committee of Publishers and Associations*

Library of Congress Cataloging-in-Publication Data

Name: Sincere, Michael, author.
Title: How to profit in the stock market / Michael Sincere.
Description: New York : McGraw Hill, [2022] | Includes bibliographical
    references and index.
Identifiers: LCCN 2021060579 (print) | LCCN 2021060580 (ebook) | ISBN
    9781264267316 (paperback) | ISBN 9781264267323 (ebook)
Subjects: LCSH: Investment analysis. | Speculation. | Stock price forecasting.
Classification: LCC HG4529 .S496 2022 (print) | LCC HG4529 (ebook) |
    DDC 332.63/2042—dc23/eng/20220127
LC record available at https://lccn.loc.gov/2021060579
LC ebook record available at https://lccn.loc.gov/2021060580

McGraw Hill books are available at special quantity discounts to use as premiums and sales promotions or for use in corporate training programs. To contact a representative, please visit the Contact Us pages at www.mhprofessional.com.

McGraw Hill is committed to making our products accessible to all learners. To learn more about the available support and accommodations we offer, please contact us at accessibility@mheducation.com. We also participate in the Access Text Network (www.accesstext.org), and ATN members may submit requests through ATN.

To my wonderful mother and father,
and my amazing dog, Chili

To Chip, who will be remembered for his sharp wit,
his love of cats, and for creating a simple
but successful commodity trading system

CONTENTS

PART FOUR
High-Risk, High-Reward Trading Strategies

PART FIVE
Corrections, Crashes, and Bear Markets

PART SIX
Selling Stocks and Options

PREFACE

What You Need to Know First

I want to thank you for taking the time to buy my book, a follow-up to my bestselling book *Understanding Stocks*. I wanted to write a book for traders and investors who are no longer beginners, which is how this book was created. In the first book, I taught you the basics, including how to buy and sell stocks and use fundamental and technical analysis.

In this book, I have taken it up a few notches, digging deeper into indicators and oscillators, exploring buying and selling tactics, and also introducing a variety of strategies aimed at sophisticated traders and investors. I am excited about writing a book for those who are looking for higher-level strategies, tools, and ideas.

Don't worry: I continue to explain the concepts in the same friendly tone and understandable language that helped make my other financial books so successful. I write this book as if we are having a conversation at the kitchen table.

WHAT YOU WILL LEARN

You are in the right place if you know the basics and want to learn more about the stock market. As always with my other books, I try to make this book educational as well as entertaining. My goal is to save you time and money while teaching you ways to increase income and build wealth.

Before writing this book, I spent years testing and evaluating the stock market. I approached the stock market like a scientist, conducting numerous experiments to determine what worked, and what didn't. As a result of my research, I was able to bring new insights and ideas to writing this book. I am very eager to share what I learned with you.

My goal is to help you gain a deeper understanding of the stock market so you can increase profits over the short or long term. I took the classes, read the books, watched the videos, and talked to dozens of pros. I also invested and traded stocks, and along the way, I've made many mistakes, which I will help you to avoid.

The bottom line is that you are reading this book because you want to make money. One of the best ways to make that happen is by participating in the stock market, as either an investor or trader. By the time you finish this book, you should have learned a variety of different methods and strategies to succeed.

STOCK MARKET RISKS

As your author, a job I take seriously, I want you to know that you need to know both the benefits and the risks of participating in the stock market. There are risks when you trade or invest, just as there are risks with anything else associated with the financial markets.

Although you can never eliminate all risks, there are ways to minimize them. That means if you lose money in the market, although painful, it won't be devastating to your portfolio. That is why learning how to limit losses is so important.

I am also realistic. Unfortunately, the market is not a fairy godmother that can solve all your financial obligations. Most of the time, stocks are an excellent investment. However, I also know that if you choose the wrong stock, or if the market drops, or if there is a correction, you can lose money.

That is why one of my main goals is to help protect your stock positions from large losses. You don't want to be a sitting duck, which is why I will show you some of the clues to look for before the market falls. I'll even show you how to profit from market pullbacks and plunges.

HOW THE BOOK IS ORGANIZED

In Part One, you learn buying strategies as well as ways to find winning stocks. In fact, the ability to find potential winners is the first step in your journey as a short-term trader or investor.

I discuss the most useful indicators and oscillators in Part Two, from moving averages to stochastics, including how they generate specific buy and sell signals. I gained additional insights by interviewing many of the creators of the most popular indicators, which I share with you.

We'll cover trend following and momentum trading strategies in Part Three. I also included specific technical signals to help with buy and sell decisions. Many traders use one or both of these strategies, which is the reason I examine both the benefits and risks of each method.

Anyone interested in high-risk, high-reward strategies will enjoy Part Four. That's when I introduce day trading, trading gaps, cryptocurrencies, and penny stocks. While these strategies are not for everyone, learning how they work may be useful. For many, they are pure entertainment.

Because a bear market, correction, or crash is always looming, I want you to be prepared. In Part Five, I share the methods you should use not only to survive during volatile market environments, but to thrive. As an added bonus, I discuss how market pros, from seasoned investors to short sellers, handle bear markets. Speaking of short selling, I show you how to do it.

Part Six addresses tactics and strategies for selling stocks and options, what I call the *art of selling*. To close out the book, I discuss how to sell covered calls. This easy-to-learn options strategy is ideal for anyone who owns stock and wants to rent that stock to others. Even if you have no interest in using options, this strategy will be there if you're looking for income and cash flow.

In closing, I offer some parting advice on what to do next, along with good sources of further information and a glossary of indicators.

NOW IS THE TIME TO GET STARTED

There has never been a better time to learn about and participate in the stock market. You have access to new technology, tools, and equipment that previous generations could only dream about.

Most importantly, by the time you finish this book, you will know when to enter and exit, when to buy and sell, and how to avoid the traps that ensnare most traders. There are many more strategies to learn, but at a minimum, my goal is to give you the information needed to succeed as a twenty-first-century trader or investor.

HOW TO CONTACT ME

Thanks again for taking the time to read my book. I appreciate that of all the books you could have chosen, you chose mine. I will do my best to make you happy with that decision.

My goal is to show you how to make a decent amount of money (a sum that varies for each person) on your own, so you don't have to rely on me or anyone else.

I also hope that I inspire you to learn more about the stock market the same way that I did. Finally, if you have questions about my book or notice any errors, feel free to e-mail me at msincere@gmail.com, or visit my website, www.michaelsincere.com. I always enjoy hearing from you, and I'll try to answer promptly.

Now let's get to work—there is a lot to learn!

HOW TO
PROFIT IN THE
STOCK MARKET

THE ART OF BUYING

I n this book, I am going to act as your personal tour guide, showing you many different paths to helping you achieve your financial goals. The first step in this process is identifying which stocks to buy.

Not everyone realizes it, but there is an art to buying stocks. The scientific aspect of the stock market is technical analysis, which you will learn about in Part Two. The "artistic" part includes not only interpreting the signals correctly but making the right trade at the right time. In Part One, I will show you many helpful tactics and strategies.

The hard part of trading is not just making a profit but keeping that profit. This is a challenge for all market participants. For example, let's say that two great stock pickers, Warren Buffett and Peter Lynch, told you that they liked a company, YYYY Manufacturing (not a real company), because its earnings were expected to substantially increase over the next several years. They recommend that you buy YYYY stock.

The next morning after the market opens, you sign into your account and buy 400 shares of YYYY. Guess what? The odds are very good that one month from today, instead of making the huge profits you dreamed about, you will have lost money. How is this possible?

This story is common among traders. Traders and investors often buy good stocks, but at the wrong time. Others buy at a good time but watch all their profits disappear because they ignored the sell signals. Others buy stocks and lose patience and sell right before the stock price takes off.

I'll tell you the truth: While it's easy to teach the scientific part of trading (technical and fundamental analysis), it's a challenge to teach how to buy and sell for profits. For example, if you get too emotionally involved with a stock or misread the technical signals, your outcome is likely to be poor.

The good news is that you can improve your trading skills with practice, and the right trading book (I wonder which one!). No one said it's easy to make a profit, but I will explain how to do so. As you'll also discover, potential winners are everywhere. The key is knowing how to separate the wheat from the chaff, the winners from the losers.

You may be asking, if it's so easy to find winners, why isn't everyone making money in the stock market? Good question. By the end of the book, I hope you will join that fortunate group of traders and investors who not only find winning stocks but also earn money from them.

And now, let's get started learning how to find winning stocks.

NOTE: I assume you already know the mechanics of how to enter orders to buy and sell stocks. If not, the step-by-step procedures are thoroughly discussed in my previous book, *Understanding Stocks*.

CHAPTER 1

FIND WINNING STOCKS

N o matter how good your strategy, equipment, or technical indicators, if you choose the wrong stock, you are likely to lose money. Therefore, one of the keys to succeeding as a trader or investor is to find a potential winner. That is what you will learn to do in this chapter, and I can't stress how important it is.

There are many ways to discover winning stocks. Most traders use technical analysis, some look at fundamental information, while others use scanning software from their brokerage. There is no best method because it's a personal choice.

Before you can find a winner, you need search criteria. Obviously, nearly all market participants have different opinions about which stocks will make it to the winner's circle. The important part is choosing the right stock at the right time. If you can do that, your chances of making money for the day, week, month, or longer are good.

On the other hand, if you choose a losing stock, no matter how skilled you are as a trader, the chances are high that you will lose money. You must also be cautious about buying stocks recommended by a know-it-all tout on TV or uninformed acquaintances. Many times, these stocks turn out to be duds. (These stocks should first be put on your *Watch List*, which you will learn about in the sidebar at the end of this chapter.)

Throughout this book, I show you various ways to find winners while avoiding losers. Often, I mention a number of trophy stocks that have performed well in the past. However, note that although learning about stocks from the past is helpful, my focus is on helping you find stocks that may succeed in the future.

As economic conditions change and the years go by, so will the list of potential winners. Many of the successful stocks mentioned in this book may fall out of favor as technology advances and economic conditions change. I encourage you to carefully consider which criteria to choose.

Don't worry if you don't know where to start. In this chapter, I give ideas of what to look for when buying stocks. The stock ideas can be used for any strategy covered in this book, including *trend*, *momentum*, *swing*, and *position* trading. Choose stocks that are suitable for the strategy and method that you use (or plan to use).

HOW TO FIND A WINNING STOCK

As you read earlier, winning stocks are everywhere. You get ideas from financial websites, magazine articles, money managers, and TV personalities who throw out dozens of stock picks. Nearly everyone has stock tips, and people freely share them with you.

Below are some of the criteria to look for when finding strong stocks that have the potential to move higher (or lower if you are betting against the market). These are the kind of stocks that both traders and investors usually want to trade.

> **NOTE:** You aren't limited to choosing stocks. For example, many traders prefer to trade ETFs (*exchange-traded funds*). The three most popular and most liquid ETFs are SPY, QQQ, and IWM, which track the S&P 500, Nasdaq, and Russell 2000,

respectively. Another choice is to trade individual sectors such as technology, retail, pharmaceuticals, or commodities.

NOTE: Although I'll show you how to find winning stocks, another idea is to use the scanning software on your broker's website to find candidates that meet the criteria that you set. You don't have any criteria? Don't worry; you will get dozens of ideas when reading about the indicators and oscillators in Part Two.

STOCK-BUYING IDEAS

The following ideas should get you started thinking about how to find winning stocks. Keep a trading diary to write down any new prospects. Some of the best ideas come from the products that you buy, the stores where you shop, and the services that you use.

Idea #1: Look for Stocks Making 52-Week Highs or Lows

One of the easiest ways to find potential winners is to look at the list of stocks making new 52-week highs or lows. These lists are in your broker's software or at numerous investment websites such as MarketWatch, Yahoo Finance, Google Finance, *Barron's*, the *Wall Street Journal*, Barchart, CNN Money, and Market Chameleon.

Stocks that are trading at or near their all-time highs get the most attention. The 52-week high list is like "bees to honey" to momentum and trend traders who often buy stocks near all-time highs. On the other hand, *contrarian* traders may bet against these same stocks.

Many institutions such as mutual funds and hedge funds are also interested in stocks that trade at one-year highs. At the end of every quarter, many managers flock to stocks making all-time or one-year highs while dumping losers. Owning winning stocks help make money managers look smart, which keeps clients happy while also attracting new money from investors.

Idea #2: Find Stocks with High Volume

Stocks powered by strong *volume* often turn into short- and long-term holdings. Volume is the fuel that forces stocks higher or lower. The higher the volume, the stronger the trend, which increases the potential that the stock is going to be a keeper.

One advantage of buying high-volume stocks is that they are *liquid* (easy to buy and sell). Liquid stocks are actively traded (1 million or more shares traded daily). On the other hand, stocks that are illiquid tend to have wider bid-ask spreads, making it difficult to get a good execution on your trade.

Therefore, look for stocks with higher-than-normal volume. The brute force of high volume makes some of these stocks unstoppable, especially during a bull market. These stocks have the potential to be big winners.

You also want to identify stocks with high "relative" volume. These are stocks whose volume has recently increased by so much that they deserve your attention. For example, if a stock that normally trades 1 million shares is now trading 10 million shares, it should be put on your Watch List. More than likely, institutions have discovered the stock. It's often a good idea to find stocks with strong institutional backing.

> **NOTE:** There are traders who have no interest in buying the "generals," that is, the most well-known and most actively traded stocks. Instead, they prefer buying lesser-known, low-priced stocks using momentum strategies.
>
> Some of these low-liquidity stocks are easy to buy but difficult to sell at a price that's good for you. Because some trad-

ers love these strategies and these stocks, I discuss the pros and cons of buying momentum stocks in Chapter 10.

Idea #3: Find Stocks Moving Higher in the Premarket

Here's a strategy: Identify stocks that are already moving higher by 1 or 2 percent (or more) in the *premarket*. Stocks that spurt out of the starting gate up by 1 or 2 percent (or 1 or 2 points for some stocks) are likely to keep moving higher all morning, and perhaps all day or longer.

There is no guarantee that they will continue to move higher after the opening bell because much depends on the overall market environment. In addition, some stocks that start off strong at the open stall and reverse direction.

It's relatively easy to identify stocks that are early winners. The hard part is finding the ones that continue trending higher all day or all week. Obviously, finding winning stocks is only your first step. You should read this entire book to learn how to enter at the right time and exit with a profit. Typically, you need technical analysis for guidance.

IMPORTANT: A stock opening higher isn't enough reason to buy it. Track the winners and try to determine which have the most potential. Under no circumstances should you *chase* stocks, especially those that move extremely high at the open (*gapping stocks*). Sometimes stocks surge higher after the market opens but stall and quickly reverse.

The main point is that stocks that start strong at the opening bell and are backed by a bullish market environment have an excellent chance of trending higher all day. These stocks are true winners, and many are unstoppable, at least for the day (and perhaps longer).

TRADING NOTE: If you decide to trade these stocks, don't make the mistake of placing a trade in the first five minutes (what traders call "amateur hour"). Because the conflicting orders at the open are so volatile, it's easy to get whipsawed, resulting in a poor fill. Buying strategies will be discussed thoroughly in Chapter 2.

NOTE: Some of the websites that list stocks moving higher or lower in the premarket include MarketWatch, CNN Money, Yahoo Finance, Google Finance, Market Chameleon, and Barchart.

Idea #4: Identify Stocks in a Trading Range

Some traders or short-term investors may want to look for stocks that move in a predictable trading range, for example, between $40 and $50 per share. With this strategy, buy when the stock moves close to the lower range (such as at $40 in this example), and reduce or sell the position at the upper range (such as at $50).

The good news is there are always stocks like these waiting to be discovered. To look for candidates, scan through long-term stock charts.

In the old days, General Electric and IBM were ideal candidates. You could buy near the bottom of a trading range and sell at the top. For years, investors could depend on stocks like these to stay in a well-defined range and not break out lower or higher.

On occasion, stocks trading in a range move much higher (they break out), delighting investors and traders alike. In recent years, stocks such as Apple, Alphabet, Netflix, and many others have broken above *resistance* and never looked back.

NOTE: Stocks that trade within a trading range have both a *support* and a *resistance* price, which we will discuss in Chapter 3.

In the example above, $40 was the support level and $50 was the resistance level. When a stock breaks above resistance, that is when many traders and investors get excited about the short- and long-term prospects of the company. Many consider it as a buying opportunity.

Idea #5: Buy the "Steady Eddies"

There is nothing more satisfying than finding a "Steady Eddie" stock that moves in a stable, relatively steady direction (typically higher) with only a few hiccups along the way. A few of the stocks that have fit this criterion are Walmart, Home Depot, Lowe's, and Johnson & Johnson. Because these stocks went higher for years, buying such stocks was a profitable venture. Steady Eddie stocks can generate consistent profits year after year.

As you read this book, be on the lookout for other stocks that have superb fundamentals and are in an uptrend. They are often well-known stocks favored by large institutions but are often not exciting enough for some retail investors.

Banks and insurance company stocks are often excellent candidates—the kind of stocks that Warren Buffett likes to buy, even if some of them may put you to sleep. Perhaps some of these stocks aren't as sexy as the "go-go" stocks favored by some traders, but as long as they keep moving higher, it's hard to go wrong owning them (especially as many also pay rich *dividends*).

CAVEAT: Although many stocks mentioned here were ideal nominees at one time, there is no guarantee they will be in the future. That is why it's important to continue looking for new candidates.

Idea #6: Find Stocks with Relative Strength

Look for individual stocks that move in a different direction from the overall market. For example, if the entire market is declining but a handful of stocks are flat or moving higher, these stocks should be put on your Watch List and monitored for possible bullish moves. Based on relative strength, these stocks have outperformed the index and probably many other securities.

To be precise, relative strength is a ratio that compares the stock price performance with an index, sector, or another stock over a given time period. A stock diverging higher from the overall market is said to have "relative strength." Put another way, the stock has outperformed the overall market or index.

Conversely, stocks moving lower from the overall market are said to have "relative weakness." It's one of the oldest ideas among traders and can lead to discovering winning stocks.

Stocks that have strong relative strength are often the first to recover when the market moves higher after a sell-off (and after the stock has bottomed). They survive the sell-off and benefit from the upside reversal. This is just one of many reasons why it's useful to understand and apply relative strength when selecting which stocks to purchase.

> **NOTE:** Do not confuse the term *relative strength* discussed above with the relative strength index (RSI), which you'll read about in Chapter 5.

Idea #7: Find Home Run Stocks

Search for stocks that, within months, have the potential to move 15 to 25 percent from entry to exit. The idea is to let one of these beauties do its magic and bloom until it fully matures.

Finding a home run stock is not easy. Such stocks are often hiding in plain sight and may not be included on the watch lists of many traders. In hindsight, one of the greatest home run trades in history was when Apple fell below $6 per share in the 1990s. After Steve Jobs triumphantly returned to create the Apple iPod, the rest is history.

Although Apple was the perfect home run stock, opportunities such as this don't come around very often. It's also not an easy trade because there was a risk that Apple was not going to recover from its debacle.

The ideal time to find a home run stock is typically after a major pullback or correction. That means searching for a seriously oversold stock that has been temporarily thumped. Find one of these "diamonds in the rough," and you have the potential to hit a home run.

This strategy is for anyone willing to wait for a rare opportunity to profit from special situations (such as when there is "blood in the streets"). While everyone else is running away in fear from the stock market, you are shopping for beaten-up stocks that are temporarily in the doghouse. Choose the right stock, and you can make substantial profits.

> **TRADING NOTE:** Once you have identified a home run candidate, and after receiving a buy signal, consider *scaling* into the trade (rather than using the lump-sum investment method). The key to success with this method is waiting for a buy signal. After buying, give the stock time to develop and mature. This is not a short-term trade but a *position trade* (holding for several months or longer). Sit and wait until your profit goals have been achieved (and if not, cut your losses).

Idea #8: Don't Forget the Fundamentals

In this book we are primarily focused on technical analysis. However, as I discussed in my companion book, *Understanding*

Stocks, I encourage you to consider assets, liabilities, and other fundamental data when searching for stock candidates.

Stocks with excellent fundamentals typically have increased sales and earnings over several years, may pay dividends, and have little or no debt. Fundamental data is available on your brokerage firm's website or on the internet sites mentioned in the Resources section at the end of the book. Often, studying fundamental information is an ideal starting place when searching for stocks to buy.

Famed mutual fund manager Peter Lynch used fundamental analysis to find reasonably priced stocks in top-notch companies. He studied a company's balance sheet to help identify companies whose stocks he wanted to own.

Lynch was always on the hunt for stocks that had the potential to return 10 times their initial cost. He called these stocks "10 baggers," a term he coined. These home run stocks have extremely strong earnings and also represent a good value.

My hope is that you now have some ideas about which stocks to buy (and in the next chapter, when we discuss technical analysis, there will be more ideas). As your list of stock candidates grows, you need to monitor them. That is why it's important to create a Watch List.

CREATE A WATCH LIST

Maintaining an up-to-date Watch List is essential to your success as a trader. It is a list of stocks, ETFs, or other securities that you follow and would consider owning. Every brokerage firm makes it easy to create one or multiple Watch Lists using its software.

For example, you could create a list of stocks in a certain sector such as technology or retail, or a list of low-priced stocks that you may want to buy, or even a list of stocks derived from tip givers (tipsters).

The first step is to add stocks that meet your criteria. The Watch List can include as few or as many stocks as you can easily monitor. Your list can range from a few dozen and up, but many professionals have lists in the hundreds.

The Watch List contains basic information such as the stock quote, volume, and other important trade details. You can view the Watch List on an iPad or other tablet, a computer, or a smartphone.

Many stocks on your Watch List will have a high correlation to the overall stock market and represent the core group of stocks that you monitor.

Another popular method of finding potential winners is using a *stock screener*. A stock screener is an excellent method to search for stocks with any technical or fundamental criteria that you enter. As you read this book, you will think of your own criteria (such as stocks that have made 52-week highs or lows).

Your broker should have a stock screener as part of its trading software. In addition, financial websites that have stock screeners include Yahoo Finance, Google Finance, Barchart, MarketWatch, Finviz, MSN Money, Market Chameleon, and others.

NOTE: Your Watch List should also include the three major indexes: Dow Jones Industrial Average (DJIA), Standard & Poor's 500 (SPX), and Nasdaq Composite Index (IXIC). At a minimum, ETFs such as SPY and QQQ should be included on your Watch List.

· · · · · · · · ·

Now that I have given you a few ideas of how to find winning stocks (and I know you will discover others), in the next chapter, I'll introduce a number of buying tactics that may be helpful.

CHAPTER 2

BUYING STRATEGIES AND TACTICS

I n this chapter, I will introduce a number of buying strategies. What is the difference between the amateur trader and a professional? The pros have trading strategies, tactics, and ideas thought out in advance. Few experienced traders make impulsive emotional purchases, and neither should you.

After finding a potential winner, many traders immediately buy the stock, sometimes within minutes after the opening bell. If you find a potential winner, don't feel like you have to buy it *right now*. If you are overwhelmed with a frantic feeling, I strongly recommend not making the trade. It is important to learn that "right now" is seldom a good time to make a new trade. If anything, it may be the right time to exit a bad trade. Any stock you buy based on fear or greed often turns into a loser.

Others are so afraid of missing out on the trade that they load the boat with as many shares as they can afford. All they can think about is the money they may lose by not making the trade. This emotional ailment, known as *FOMO* (fear of missing out), is common with anxious traders.

To help you with the buying decision, the following are three buying strategies. Choose the ones that make the most sense to you. The first buying idea, scaling into an investment, is a clever way of buying without making huge bets. This is one way to minimize risk.

IDEA #1: SCALING INTO AN INVESTMENT

After deciding that a stock is worth buying, many traders use the lump-sum investment method. They buy as many shares as they can afford to (or want to) buy. For example, they may buy 1,000 shares of a stock at one time. While this method has some advantages, dropping a fistful of dollars on any old stock can be risky, especially if the stock moves in the wrong direction.

A more strategic buying method is *scaling* into an investment. For example, let's say that you are interested in buying XYZ. Instead of investing $1,000 at one time, consider investing $200 in XYZ at first. Put another way, you "stagger" the purchases over a short or long time period using only a portion of your capital with each installment.

After making that initial purchase, sit back and see how the stock performs. I recommend that you give the stock some time to simmer before adding additional shares. If the stock price doesn't budge, let it marinate before adding to the position.

Scaling into a trade is a powerful risk management method, one you should consider using. Although you can't control stock prices, you do have control over the size of your trade.

This is one of your best weapons to control risk.

Scaling into Winners

If the stock in the example above moves higher after you buy it, feel free to spend another $200 at an "appropriate" time (read the next section for more specific advice). This buying strategy involves scaling into winners as they move higher.

Scaling into winners is distasteful to many traders whose mantra is to "buy low and sell high." The idea of buying at higher prices goes against everything these traders were taught. If you can't stand to buy stocks at higher prices, then you may not like this scaling method. Nevertheless, I recommend seriously considering it.

Scaling Higher Tactics

If you use the "scaling higher" method mentioned above, you may wonder when you should add to your position. That is an excellent question. In fact, the most important trade when scaling higher is not the first trade: It is the second trade. It will determine the success or failure of your strategy. Be sure that any additional purchases are strategic and not random.

The first trade is easier because it is made when the stock is on its way higher. The hope is, the stock continues moving up (and if not, quickly cut your losses at a predetermined price). As long as the stock rises steadily, slowly scale into the position.

If you are right about the stock price direction, then your position will be profitable. As the stock moves higher, there will be a point when you should stop scaling in (this is the tricky part). One such time occurs when you are fully invested—that is, the $1,000 you allocated for this position has been invested.

In other words, don't mindlessly scale in whenever you feel like it, but do so based on a plan. The last thing you want to do is add to a winning position that is *overbought* and at risk of reversing. This is the so-called bull trap, a painful experience that bullish traders want to avoid.

Don't Scale into Losers

If the stock you just bought takes a turn in the wrong direction, you'll be glad that you committed only $200 to this position (in this example). Instead of losing $1,000, you limited the loss to only $200.

> **IMPORTANT:** If your initial purchase loses money, don't buy more shares. Adding to a losing position is what is known as "trying to catch a falling knife," something you don't want to do. Remind yourself with this saying: Only losers add to losers.

IDEA #2: BUYING THE DIP

Many traders love "buying the dip," or buying stocks as prices decline, hoping to make a purchase at the lowest possible price. This strategy is taught at many finance schools and is recommended in many books and on numerous websites. After all, buying low and selling high is the goal of many connected to the financial markets.

For buying the dip to work, you must have a plan, strategy, or system. The market is mad enough: Don't add to the craziness by buying without a strategy.

Some of the best dip-buying candidates are stocks that you know and have been watching for weeks, months, or years. When one of the stocks on your Watch List has a setback, some traders buy the dip. Did I say this was easy? No. It takes some probing to get it right.

Sure, sometimes impulsive buyers get lucky and make a profit on a spontaneous buy-the-dip purchase, but one day their luck may run out. That is why it's so important to have a well-thought-out plan.

REMINDER: If you're going to buy the dip, use the scaling strategy discussed earlier. Rather than buying with one lump sum, stagger your purchase over a short time period.

When the Dip Keeps Dipping

One of the problems with the buy-the-dip strategy is when the dipping stock doesn't reverse but keeps falling. Before you know it, you could be painfully behind on the trade.

That's when many amateurs refuse to sell or even add to the losing position. Some started off as traders and switch to being "stuck-holders" when the stock doesn't recover. In some cases, they are stuck in the losing position for years.

Some traders justify the losing trade by claiming they are "dollar-cost averaging," that is, investing a set amount of money for a set time period over the long term. I'm sorry, but you can't switch from a dip buyer to dollar-cost averaging unless you're afflicted with a bad case of "hopium."

Here's some advice: If a trade is going against you, stop buying the dip and exit. Don't throw good money after bad.

NOTE: Keep in mind that buying the dip is a market-timing strategy designed to take advantage of short-term pullbacks. The trader's plan is to profit from the sale price and accumulate additional stock. Dips may not last long, so waiting for an even lower price may not be a good idea.

When Buying the Dip Stops Working

Buying the dip works because the market trends higher most of the time. Unfortunately, it won't work well during a long-term bear market. If you buy the dip during a downtrending market, you may wish you hadn't.

When the market sells off, there is a flood of financial experts telling you to buy the dip because stocks are "on sale." Others announce that stocks "are too cheap to sell!"

Let me be clear: There is nothing wrong with buying the dip, but do it right. Use the tools and strategies that are included in this book. This is a better method than playing it by ear, listening to tip givers, or making impulsive trades.

> **NOTE:** The brilliant financier and trader Bernard Baruch once quipped, "Don't try to buy at the bottom or sell at the top. It can't be done—except by liars." He once said the secret to his stock market success was that he always bought too late and sold too early.
>
> I mention this only to help you think differently about the market. Just because the majority on Wall Street tells you to buy low and sell high (buy the dip), that doesn't mean it is correct.

IDEA #3: BUYING HIGH AND SELLING HIGHER

Those who love to buy the dip may be repelled by this popular trend-following strategy: buying high and selling higher. Buying high works as long as you don't cross over the line to "chasing," which is easy to do. By the end of this book, the distinction will be clear. If you make the mistake of chasing, the financial pain could be severe.

If your plan is to buy stocks as they move higher, add stocks that are at or near their 52-week highs to your Watch List. The idea is to ride the wave of a strong uptrend. Sometimes, specific stocks keep moving higher for days, weeks, months, and even years. If you can catch one of these winners, you'll be in good shape for a long time, depending on your trading strategy.

The Risks of Buying High

When buying stocks at their highs, in a way you are rolling the dice and hoping the upward momentum continues. If it does, then the strategy works brilliantly.

On the other hand, when stocks are in "rarefied" overbought territory, any negative news or other hiccups can send the stocks reeling backward. It takes a strong belief in the strategy and in the stock to hold when *short sellers* are licking their chops, ready to pounce on a stock that has moved too far and too fast and is at risk of reversing direction.

While it is wonderful to buy winning stocks at their highs and to see them moving higher, be sure to limit risk. That means not accumulating too many shares no matter how much you love the stock or its story.

> **NOTE:** To stay out of trouble, always think about risk first and reward second. That means waiting for a good entry point (by using technical analysis). The goal is to be a more strategic trader than the quickest trader in the market.

WARNING: DO NOT DOUBLE DOWN

Do you want to lose all your money really fast? Then follow the tactics of amateur traders who attempt to increase their risk and profits by doubling their bets. When right, they feel like geniuses. When wrong, they lose big-time. Based on probabilities, the odds are not in your favor when using the double-down strategy.

Even worse, some traders bet more than they can afford on a position they are certain will be a winner. Sometimes they win, sometimes they lose, but over the long term the chances are good they will get wiped out. Betting the farm on one position is not trading—it's gambling. Another hazardous-to-your-wealth strategy includes plunging into a position in an effort to get rich fast.

Infamous trader Jesse Livermore plunged multiple times, one of the reasons he went bankrupt on three occasions. Ultimately, he tripled down on the short side of the market in October 1929, and this time he was on the winning side, earning over $100 million in one week after the market crashed. It was his greatest payday, making him one of the richest men in the world.

The problem was that he couldn't stop doubling down. Livermore continued to plunge into stocks and commodities using this highly risky strategy, even though he was one of the best stock pickers in the world. After plunging one too many times, within five years all his money had disappeared.

NOTE: Doubling down is for gamblers, not traders. While the payoff can be amazing when you're right, it may wipe out your account if wrong. It's almost always a mistake to rely on Lady Luck to make money in the stock market.

THE POWER OF THE PROBE

An idea I took from Livermore's approach was to test, or *probe*, whether a stock was a good investment. Similar to scaling, the idea is to test the stock with a small initial purchase. If the trade is successful, you add to the position.

Here is the difference between scaling and probing: With scaling, your investments are spread out evenly over time. With probing, you follow up with a larger investment after the first probe is successful.

Probing is actually an excellent way to test the waters while keeping risk at a minimum. Livermore probed on the short side for months before the stock market crashed in 1929. When his short probes finally turned profitable, he dived into the market on margin, and the rest is stock market history.

One of the reasons that probing makes sense is that you are risking less money to find a winning stock and a good entry point. As long as you realize that getting the "perfect" price is unattainable, probing solves the dual dilemma of buying too early or buying too late.

RISK-REWARD CALCULATION

Before making a trade, it's a good idea to calculate a risk-reward ratio. A good guideline is one part risk to two parts reward (1:2), and one part risk to three parts reward (1:3) is even better (a 1:3 risk-reward ratio means you are risking $1 to potentially make $3).

This method requires establishing an entry price, a stop-loss price, and a price target for the stock. You cannot choose random prices; there must be some rationale behind selecting the profit target.

For example, you buy XYZ Manufacturing at $50 per share. With a 1:3 risk-reward, you plan to sell when the profit reaches $3 per share. To initiate this strategy, you enter two orders: a GTC (good 'til canceled) sell order at $53, which locks in the potential gain, and a GTC stop-loss order at $49, thereby limiting the loss to $1 per share. Here's what this trading plan looks like:

- Entry price: $50
- Stop-loss order: $49
- Profit target: $53

NOTE: The risk-reward calculation is flexible depending on the strategy used. Traders should calculate the risk-reward ratio before beginning a trade as one method for deciding whether the trade is worthwhile.

TEST BEFORE BUYING

Now that you have learned a few buying strategies (and you can look forward to learning more throughout this book), you may want to consider using your broker's software to make practice trades.

I am a believer in making practice trades in a *paper money* or *simulated trading account*. You can use the broker's software to make practice trades and test which strategies work—or don't work. It can also help sharpen your trading skills.

Would you let someone pilot an airplane before using a simulated program? Of course not. Before making real trades, it's a good idea to use a test account to explore the brokerage software. Becoming familiar with the brokerage's trading platform cuts the probability of making trading mistakes (pressing the wrong button or entering the wrong stock symbol, for example). Although not everyone is a fan of this method, the benefits far outweigh the negatives.

NOTE: If your brokerage doesn't offer a paper money account, you can find a simulated trading program on the internet. An excellent free simulated program is at the following website: platform.thinkorswim.com. You are allowed to practice using the thinkorswim software from TD Ameritrade for 60 days at no cost. Anyone in the world can use the software. Call the brokerage firm for specific instructions on using the software.

Interactive Brokers also provides a free and powerful simulated trading program that is available to traders (even if you don't have an account). Go to the company's website, www.interactivebrokers.com, for details.

Other brokerage firms that offer paper money trading programs include TradeStation, E*Trade, and Webull. According to my sources, more brokerage firms will be offering simulated trading programs in the future. Why? Because customers are demanding it.

In addition to brokerage firms, MarketWatch has a simulated trading game through its "virtual stock exchange," with a 15-minute quote delay and $100,000 in play money.

Investopedia also allows you to set up a trading game with $1 million in play money and a 15-minute quote delay.

NOTE: You should know that some traders are not fans of practice trading. The criticism is this: When real money is not at risk, you do not experience the pain of losses. Therefore, a reasonable alternative is to trade 10 to 20 percent of your normal share position (i.e., trade small).

MARKET OR LIMIT ORDER?

Although I thoroughly discussed *market orders*, *limit orders*, *stop losses*, and *time stops* in my previous book, I believe a quick review is appropriate here, especially if you are new to the stock market.

Market Order Versus Limit Order

A market order is similar to going to a car dealer and paying the list price. That means no negotiation, no haggling, and no complications. You get the car at a price that is best for the dealer. The advantage is that you get the car immediately.

It's the same with stocks. When buying a stock using a market order, you pay the lowest listed asking price without making any effort to pay less. You get the stock quickly with no negotiation.

Generally, it's better to buy stocks (or a car) with a limit order. That leaves you in control of the order so you can name your own price. At the time the order is entered, you can select a minimum selling price or a maximum purchase price. Much of the time that price is between the bid and ask.

Perhaps the main reason people use a market order is they want to be triple certain that the order is filled immediately. Maybe they are so excited to own the stock that the price they pay is unimportant. In those circumstances, a market order is appropriate.

For everyone else who doesn't want to pay the "list" price of any item, then selecting a limit order is the best choice when buying or selling.

. . . .

Now that you have learned a variety of buying strategies, it's time to turn the page and discuss technical indicators and oscillators. In the next chapter, you will learn about some of the most useful technical indicators and oscillators on the planet. They will help you with the buying and selling decisions.

TECHNICAL INDICATORS
AND OSCILLATORS

I f you read my previous book, *Understanding Stocks*, you already know the basics of technical analysis. In Part Two of this book, I go beyond the basics to teach you how to use the following indicators and oscillators: moving averages, MACD, RSI, Bollinger Bands, stochastics, and candlesticks. These are what I consider the best of the best.

In addition to learning how to use these tools to their fullest potential, I include a number of tips, insights, and ideas I have learned from the experts, including the creators of several of these indicators. As always, I share both the benefits and the limitations of these technical tools.

You have a choice: use indicators and oscillators to gain an edge or rely on your hunches about what to buy and when to sell. Although it takes more work, using indicators and oscillators is a much better use of your time.

Not using indicators is similar to flying an airplane without instruments. It can be done, but it adds unnecessary risk. Obviously, technical analysis is not the Holy Grail (or it would be the only method). Nevertheless, these tools provide valuable information and should be considered. Many traders use them as risk management and timing tools.

Let's begin with one of the most powerful and widely used indicators: moving averages.

CHAPTER 3

MOVING AVERAGES

M oving averages (MAs), along with *support* and *resistance*, are at the heart of technical analysis. In fact, using moving averages is the most popular method of evaluating stocks.

In this chapter, I explain how to use moving averages as well as support and resistance to make actionable trades. Even professional traders, especially trend followers at major financial institutions, look at these important concepts. Moving averages are essential because they keep traders on the right side of a trend. Many use moving averages to help with timing entries and exits.

If you are not familiar with moving averages, the sidebar below includes a brief introduction.

THE BASICS: MOVING AVERAGES

Moving averages are simple to use and interpret and are designed to give significant signals. Even fundamental investors who don't usually pay attention to technical indicators pay attention to moving averages, especially to the almighty 200-day moving average.

Moving averages show the value of a security's closing price over a certain time period, such as the last 20, 50, 100, or 200 days. By laying the moving average on top of a stock or index, you can identify market direction.

The average is "moving" because every day, the oldest data point is removed and replaced with the most current. To be technical, the moving average is calculated by taking the average closing price over the last 50 days (or another set number of days). This means that as the fifty-first day is added, the first day is dropped.

The data is constantly changing, and thus it is called a *moving* average. By repeating this process every day, a smooth line is created on the chart. Trend followers prefer to follow moving averages because they can quickly identify the trend's direction and detect potential reversals.

Traders use moving averages to help decide when to buy or sell. For example, short-term traders may use the 14- and 20-day moving averages on a daily chart to look for signals. A swing trader may use the 50-day moving average.

Long-term investors tend to use the popular but slow 200-day moving average for buy and sell signals. Although the 200-day moving average gives infrequent signals, when this moving average is penetrated, traders pay close attention.

For example, a simple but effective trading system that has worked for decades is buying the indexes when they move *above* their 200-day moving averages and selling when they drop *below*. Although this simple strategy has generated consistent profits in the past, there is no guarantee it will work in the future.

While you should not base all trading decisions solely on moving averages (or any other technical indicator), this indicator is still one of the most effective ever created. If I were forced to choose one indicator to help with trading decisions, I would choose moving averages.

Simple or Exponential Moving Average

The two most widely used moving averages are the *simple* and *exponential*. According to technicians, the exponential tends to be more *price sensitive* because the most recent closing prices carry a heavier weighting.

On the other hand, the simple moving average is a little slower to respond to market volatility because the closing prices are weighted equally. Put another way, each closing price is treated the same.

The most popular moving average is the simple moving average, primarily because it is the default setting on most chart programs. More than likely, the simple moving average will meet your needs. If you have time, try both moving average types to see which one generates the most useful signals for your trading style. Then use only one (and not both) for your decision-making.

· · · · · · · · ·

Figure 3.1 is a three-month chart of the Dow Jones Industrial Average (DJIA) as it falls below and then rises above its 20-, 50-, and 100-day moving averages.

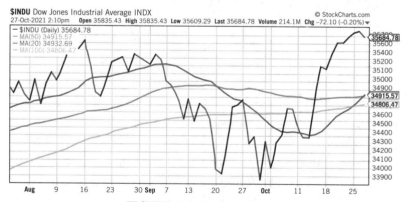

FIGURE 3.1   Moving averages
(Chart courtesy of StockCharts.com.)

Now that you have a basic understanding of moving averages, I want to show you how to generate actionable signals. If done correctly, that should lead to increased profits. As mentioned before, moving averages are designed to keep you on the right side of the trend.

1. **Buy.** If the index or stock crosses *above* its 50-, 100-, or 200-day moving average and remains above, that is considered a buy signal. Use other indicators to confirm the signal.
2. **Sell.** If the index or stock crosses below its 50-, 100-, or 200-day moving average and remains *below*, that is considered a sell signal. Again, use other indicators to confirm the signal.

HOW TRADERS USE MOVING AVERAGES

Short-term traders may prefer to use a shorter-term moving average such as the 14- or 20-day moving average because it generates early signals. Keep in mind that seeing more frequent signals doesn't mean they will turn into winning trades. If anything, the odds are high there will be a steady diet of false signals.

Swing traders (who buy and sell within 3 to 5 days) may use the 50-day moving average on a daily price chart. The 50-day moving average acts as a line in the sand and is an early warning indicator. If the stock price remains above the 50-day moving average, swing traders tend to hold long positions. However, when the stock price drops below the 50-day moving average, some traders sell their positions.

Long-term investors tend to use the 100- or 200-day moving average on both the daily and weekly chart for signals. They will buy when the stock rises above its moving average and remains above it, and sell when the stock drops below and remains below it.

HINT: The weekly stock chart gives a smoother, less volatile signal.

Sometimes a stock breaks hard below its moving averages, unleashing a flood of selling. Once the moving average falls below the 20-day moving average, if the price keeps falling, it's likely that the 50-day moving average will be threatened next. Likewise, although it takes a longer time, the 100-day moving average may also come under pressure. Each situation is different and depends on the stock's price history.

The break through a moving average is not always a slam-dunk trade, but there are important clues. For example, if a stock breaks below its 200-day moving average with heavy volume and stays below, and the slope of the moving average pivots lower, many traders consider that to be a confirmed sell signal.

This is the artistic part of trading, as traders each have their own set of guidelines. One of the main reasons to follow indicators such as moving averages is to help a trader make unemotional trading decisions, thereby managing risk more efficiently.

NOTE: Day traders tend to use much shorter time periods for moving averages. For example, they may use the 20- or 50-day moving average on a 5-minute, 15-minute, or 60-minute chart. My advice is to keep it simple until you find a moving average time period that fits your trading style and strategy.

MOVING AVERAGES DON'T PREDICT: THEY LAG

Although moving averages are powerful, they are not crystal balls and therefore can't predict the future. In fact, moving averages are considered to be a "lagging" indicator. While they do give actionable signals, they are often late to the party. When a stock is in an uptrend and moving higher, that doesn't mean the trend will continue.

NOTE: If you want to identify potential reversals with greater conviction, use indicators such as *stochastics* (explained in Chapter 7).

THE SLOPE OR STEEPNESS OF THE TREND

A lot of traders don't pay enough attention to the slope or angle of the moving average, but they should. The slope reflects whether the trend can be sustained or if a reversal is likely.

For example, look to see whether the angle or slope of one moving average is steep while another is flatlining. This suggests that momentum is declining and the stock price may reverse. Risk-averse traders may want to sell early.

If the slope of the moving average steepens dramatically, don't be surprised if the stock "falls off a cliff." It's risky to go long when a stock is in a potential death spiral. As traders often remind themselves: Don't try to catch a falling knife.

Conversely, if the slope is nearly vertical, it would be financial malpractice to sell the stock short (bet money that the stock will fall). The underlying security will eventually exhaust itself and reverse, but until then, avoid shorting any stock that behaves like a rocket ship.

THE MOVING AVERAGE CROSSOVER STRATEGY

When a stock (or index) crosses above or below one or more of its moving averages, that may be construed as a valid buy or sell signal. Specifically, when two moving averages cross, some professional traders choose to sell.

For example, when the 50-day moving average crosses *below* the 200-day moving average, that forms a bearish technical trigger known as the superstitious-sounding "Death Cross."

The Death Cross

According to financial sources, the Death Cross has been a rather reliable indicator, predicting some of the worst market sell-offs in history including 1929, 1938, 1974, and 2008.

It doesn't mean this rare signal is 100 percent accurate. Therefore, when this ominous pattern appears, it's always wise to confirm with other indicators before making any impulsive selling decisions.

Even if you aren't superstitious, if a Death Cross suddenly appears on your chart (and it will be big news in the financial media), you may want to knock on wood and stay away from mirrors before trading that day. It never hurts to take precautions—just in case the Death Cross warnings are genuine.

> **NOTE:** The bullish long-term signal is the "Golden Cross," which occurs when the 50-day moving average crosses *above* the 200-day moving average.

> **NOTE:** If you see one of these crossovers take shape, begin by looking at the slopes, which may be even more significant than the crossover. If the slope of the Death Cross is mildly bearish, you can still hold your position, but keep a close eye out for anything extraordinary.

POWERFUL BUT IMPERFECT

Although moving averages are a powerful tool, don't put all your hopes and dreams into this one indicator. It's easy to enter too early or too late, or misread the signals. The solution is having a confluence of indicators, because together they provide a more accurate view of where your stock was in the past and clues to where it may be in the future.

Bestselling author and trader Toni Turner put it this way: "Indicators are like different instruments playing in a symphony orchestra. Although all the instruments are different, when you listen to them, they all come out as a musical piece. But if even one of the instruments is playing out of tune, that is a signal you should pay attention to."

> **HINT:** Now that you know a lot more about moving averages, you may want to scan through your stock positions (or potential positions) and see how they stack up against their moving averages.

SUPPORT AND RESISTANCE

There are specific prices on a stock chart where buying or selling activity in a stock or index makes it difficult for the stock to penetrate that level. The stock could break through the price level or reverse direction.

Those prices are known as *support* and *resistance*. Think of support as a "floor" and resistance as a "ceiling." When a stock trades at or near support, buyers who remember that this price held (the stock price did not go lower) might act on the belief that this price will hold again. Thus, more buyers than usual show up to *purchase* shares. As long as these buyers are not overwhelmed by sellers, support holds and the stock does not go lower.

Conversely, when a stock trades at or near resistance, traders who believe this price will hold show up to *sell* shares. As long as these sellers are not overwhelmed by buyers, resistance holds and the stock does not go higher, or is repelled.

Example: You own 100 shares of YYYY that is trading at $44 per share. On the chart, YYYY has tried to rise above $44 per share at least three times. Each time, it has failed. Technicians say that $44 is a *resistance* level. Because YYYY was unable to move above $44 previously, the rally may "run out of gas" again and is at risk of reversing.

On the other hand, if YYYY suddenly falls to a zone where it previously was unable to penetrate, that price is a *support* level. For example, if YYYY fell to $40 per share at least two times and was unable to fall further, then $40 becomes support. If the stock price can hold support at $40 per share, that is a positive sign. Some traders may consider that price to be a short-term buy signal with $44 as the target.

NOTE: Most technicians use moving averages and trendlines to identify support and resistance. Often, the 50- 100-, and 200-day moving averages act as major support and resistance levels.

HINT: Support and resistance often occur at whole numbers. The theory is that retail investors and traders typically enter orders to buy and sell at whole numbers out of convenience.

Because so many stock prices are clustered around whole numbers, these prices can act as a ceiling and floor. Much of this is Psychology 101, which is why many people take profits at round numbers, or buy at round numbers.

You can use this clue to gain an edge over other traders. How? When it's time to place your orders, use less obvious price points that are a few pennies removed from whole numbers.

THE BATTLE FOR CONTROL

Another way to think about support and resistance is as a battle for control of the stock price. At support, there are more buyers than sellers and thus greater demand for the stock, so support tends to hold. At resistance, there are more sellers than buyers and thus a greater supply of the stock, so resistance often holds. In both situations, the stock may reverse direction.

Short-term traders constantly scan charts to determine whether a stock breaks through or holds support. When technicians notice that the stock price breaks below support, they often reduce risk by selling all or some of their long positions.

Conversely, when a stock rises above (or breaks through) resistance, and stays above, it tends to be a significant buy signal. It means the buying pressure is so strong that it overwhelms sellers. When technicians notice that the stock price broke above resistance, they may scale into the trade with buy orders.

Traders must also be alert to "head fakes" (also known as "false breakouts"). For example, when a stock price breaks through resistance and appears to be unstoppable, some impatient traders gobble up shares, assuming the stock will keep moving higher.

Not long after they press the Enter key, the stock unexpectedly reverses direction and moves lower. This happens often enough to be a problem. Fortunately, using stop orders and technical indicators for your trades helps to reduce the number of head fakes.

OBSERVE TRADING VOLUME

Another factor to consider is daily trading *volume*, or the total quantity of shares that traded on any given day. As you know, volume is displayed by a vertical histogram bar at the bottom of any stock chart.

Using volume to confirm the breakout is a good idea. It's possible that you may miss out on some profitable trades when volume does not confirm the breakout, but it also helps you to avoid a number of bad trades.

The heavier the volume, the more significant the signal. In other words, if support holds at $40 per share and volume is higher than normal, it would be unwise to make a bearish bet before the price breaks support. The bleeding has stopped for now, and the odds are good that the stock price will bounce higher.

> **HINT:** Be sure to include volume as part of any analysis because it indicates the strength or weakness of the trend. At key price levels, herd mentality typically kicks in as buyers and sellers battle for control.

DRAWING TRENDLINES

One simple way to identify a trend's direction (up, down, or sideways) is to draw trendlines using a drawing tool on the brokerage software. Beginners tend to use the "eye test," which works but is less than ideal.

The mistake that many investors and traders make is not paying attention when a trendline is broken. It is an important red flag that something has changed with the stock or market. It could even be a "get out now" signal.

Pay attention to stock prices when they drop below key price levels. Once a price violates support and the trend changes direction, it may be time to exit the position while you still have a chance. The reasons behind the stock's decline are not important to followers of technical analysis. The only thing that matters is what they see on a stock chart.

· · · · · · · ·

I hope that you found this discussion on moving averages (and support and resistance) helpful. Now we will step it up a notch and learn about one of the most powerful technical indicators ever devised, and a trader favorite: MACD (moving average convergence divergence).

CHAPTER 4

MACD

I f you ask most traders to name their top five favorite indicators, MACD (moving average convergence divergence) is consistently at the top of the list. In fact, many believe that MACD is one of the most useful indicators ever created.

In this chapter I discuss a number of creative ways to use this powerful and versatile indicator. I will also introduce the MACD Histogram.

THE BASICS: MACD

MACD, designed by Gerald Appel in the 1970s, is a trend-following price momentum indicator that helps traders determine when a trend along with its associated momentum (directional speed and duration) emerges, gains traction, ebbs, or may even reverse direction.

Be aware that MACD is a "lagging" or "backward-looking" indicator, which means that its signals confirm long-term trends but cannot make predictions. That does not diminish the value of its signals. In fact, when MACD yields a signal, it is often significant. Many short-term traders view MACD on both the daily and weekly chart.

One of the reasons that so many traders like MACD is that it's a combination trend-following and momentum indicator. It identi-

fies changes in momentum, strength, trend direction, and the duration of that trend. Best of all, it generates buy and sell triggers with
uncanny accuracy. Many traders use it to warn of trend reversals.

> **HINT:** The longer the time frame, the more significant the
> results. Many traders apply the weekly MACD to generate sig-
> nals. Short-term traders tend to prefer the more price-sensitive
> daily MACD.

How MACD Works

MACD can be found as part of any charting package. When displayed on a chart, there are two lines. Watch how the lines interact
with, converge with, and diverge against each other. They do all these
things but at different speeds (one line is faster than the other).

The black line is referred to as the MACD line. The red line
(which is gray on many computer screens) is referred to as the 9-day
signal line. In addition, there is a horizontal line that runs across the
chart, which is referred to as the zero line (0 line). Keep your eyes
on the MACD line because it generates the most important signals.

The default settings are the 12-day simple moving average, the
26-day simple moving average, and a 9-day signal line (12, 26, 9).
Figure 4.1 shows what MACD looks like on a daily chart using the
default settings of 12, 26, 9.

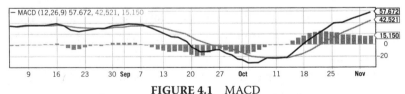

FIGURE 4.1 MACD
(Chart courtesy of StockCharts.com.)

Figure 4.1 shows a bullish setup for the underlying security, SPX. MACD is above the zero line, which is bullish. MACD has also crossed over the 9-day signal line, another bullish signal. This is a very bullish chart.

Here are a few of the signals to look for when using MACD:

- **Bullish.** When the MACD line (the black line) crosses above the zero line, the primary trend of the underlying security is bullish.
- **Bearish.** When the MACD line crosses below the zero line, the primary trend of the underlying security is bearish.
- **Bullish.** When the MACD line crosses above the 9-day signal line, the secondary trend (and short-term momentum) is bullish.
- **Bearish.** When the MACD line crosses below the 9-day signal line, the secondary trend (and short-term momentum) is bearish.
- **Actionable signals.** When both the MACD line and 9-day signal line move in the same direction (uptrend or downtrend), that is a strong signal. Nevertheless, use another indicator to confirm.
- **Divergent signals.** When the stock price moves in a different direction from MACD, that's *divergence*. For example, if the stock price moves lower, but the MACD line is moving higher, the downtrend has not been validated. Also, when the stock price makes a new high but MACD moves lower, that is a warning sign. These are guidelines, of course, not definitive rules.

IMPORTANT CAVEAT: Just because MACD generates a buy or sell signal does not mean it is an actionable trade. Like that of any other indicator, there are false signals.

How to Get the Most Out of MACD

You already know that MACD is a momentum indicator (among other things). Here's something that many traders don't know: The greater the separation between the MACD line and the signal line, the greater the momentum. The closer the lines come together, the less the momentum.

Because momentum always changes before prices change, the *MACD histogram* is especially valuable in determining a possible trend change. (The MACD histogram will be introduced next.)

Nobody's Perfect

While MACD works brilliantly during most market environments, it doesn't work as well when volatility is low. Because it's a momentum indicator, when momentum is weak and volatility is low, MACD is not as effective (you can look at the VIX for clues about volatility). As veteran trader Jeff Bierman warns, "Low volatility and poor liquidity is kryptonite to MACD."

If MACD flatlines and signals are not as useful, switch to other types of momentum indicators until volatility returns. Fortunately, MACD works extremely well with individual stocks as long as they are volatile.

Finally, as with any other indicator, MACD may give false signals. That is one reason to use MACD with a weekly time period. The weekly tends to yield fewer false signals compared with the daily.

> **HINT:** Another limitation of MACD is that it doesn't work as well at market (or stock) tops but tends to work best at bottoms.

INTRODUCING THE MACD HISTOGRAM

One of the most powerful (but often ignored) oscillators is the *MACD histogram*, which helps gauge momentum. Created by Thomas Aspray in 1986, this oscillator moves above or below the zero line. It is a separate software program from MACD but should be available on your chart package.

If you've never used the histogram, you're in for a treat. Traders who use this feature typically have both MACD and the histogram on the chart simultaneously. Here's how it works:

After selecting MACD histogram, you should see a series of green or red bar graphs on the bottom of the screen. If the bars move *above* the zero line, it means the underlying stock is gaining strength (momentum). If the bars move *below* the zero line, the stock is building selling momentum. Higher bars mean stronger bullish momentum, while lower bars mean greater bearish momentum.

> **NOTE:** What if the stock price is higher but the histogram is negative? Many traders view that as a warning sign. Cautious traders should consider waiting before taking a position (while this is not a rule, it is an important guideline).

Figure 4.2 shows the MACD histogram for an individual stock. The stock rallied in September until MACD crossed below the 9-day signal line, a bearish signal. The MACD histogram turned negative, and the stock dropped. In December, MACD rose above the zero line, and the histogram turned positive. The stock rallied back to its old highs.

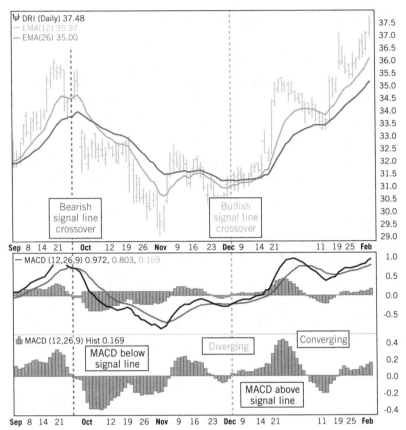

FIGURE 4.2 MACD histogram
(Chart courtesy of StockCharts.com.)

Important Signals

- If the MACD histogram bars rise *above* the zero line, that is a buy signal. When the histogram bars fall *below* the zero line, that is a sell signal.

  HINT: Watch the bars carefully for clues. Remember, if the bars are rising (getting taller) above the zero line, that is considered a bullish sign. If the bars are shrinking below the zero line, that is considered a bearish sign. In either case, a trend change is possible.

- When the MACD histogram bar color changes to a lighter shade (from dark green to light green or dark red to light red), it means that momentum is diminishing. It's not necessarily a sell signal—it shows only that buying enthusiasm has eased. It's also not a sell-short signal for the bears; it only shows that selling pressure has lightened.

    It's similar to a car reducing speed but still moving in the same direction. More than likely, stock prices will follow the decreased momentum lower. Watch for signs of a reversal.

    In addition, if the MACD histogram bar color changes to a darker shade (from light green to dark green or light red to dark red), it means that momentum is increasing. Again, it's not necessarily a buy signal; it only shows that buying enthusiasm has escalated.

HINT: As mentioned earlier, many beginners don't realize that momentum always changes before prices. That is what makes the MACD histogram valuable as a momentum indicator. When the histogram bars move below zero as the stock rises, it is a red flag. This phenomenon is known as *bearish divergence*, which tends to lead to a price breakdown.

However, if the stock is falling while the histogram bars are growing taller, this is known as *bullish divergence*, which may foreshadow an imminent rally. The price is moving lower, and the bullish momentum is strengthening.

Trade Example Using the MACD Histogram

Let's say that YYYY has been lower for five consecutive days. You believe the stock is *oversold*, so you plan to buy shares. By looking at a stock chart, there is no way to predict how low YYYY will fall. Fighting the downtrend is risky, especially as YYYY keeps falling.

Looking at the MACD histogram a few days later, you notice that the histogram has turned from red to green. This does not mean it's safe to go long. It does mean that momentum has increased.

It's a personal decision what to do next. Look at the stock price and see if the decline has stalled. If both the stock price and the MACD histogram are strengthening, that is a clue that the stock may reverse to the upside.

> **NOTE:** The signal is stronger if both the histogram and the stock price are moving in the same direction. It still makes sense to confirm what you see on the chart with other indicators, providing a more balanced perspective.

> **REMINDER:** When the MACD histogram bars change colors and get shorter, momentum is weakening. On the other hand, when the bars lengthen, momentum is strengthening.

INTERVIEW WITH MACD'S CREATOR: GERALD APPEL

There is no better way to learn about an indicator than to talk to the person who conceived it. A few years ago, when writing my book *All About Market Indicators* (McGraw Hill), I had the pleasure of speaking with MACD's creator, the late Gerald Appel. In the late 1970s, Appel created what he called moving average convergence divergence, or MACD.

Because the personal computer hadn't been created yet, Appel and his friends used a punch machine to manually enter the data into a spreadsheet. By 1980 he was able to automate the process using computer software.

Appel was surprised that MACD became so popular with traders. He believed its popularity could be traced to its flexibility. "It works because it's adaptable to any time frame," he said. "You can get a good reading of the major trend of the market by using MACD patterns that are based on monthly data. You can also use it on a five-minute chart."

Appel explained the math behind the indicator: "MACD was created by subtracting a shorter-term exponential moving average from a longer-term one. And then it uses the moving average of that. You can see when the trends are crossing their own moving average."

He said that MACD gives the most precise signals at market bottoms. "It's more accurate at market low points than high points because of the way the market behaves," he said. "You can see it easily and readily. Market bottoms tend to be very sharp and pronounced while tops can be a bit tricky."

He continued: "At bottoms, it makes very smooth lines, and you usually have climaxes and sharp reversals. It's a whole different feeling. A bear market can end on a dime, but a bull market doesn't. Market tops tend to be broad and slow. It's very possible for the market averages to keep drifting upward while more and more stocks are falling."

Almost Perfect

Although MACD is an excellent indicator, Appel warned that it was not perfect. "No indicator is infallible," he said. "For instance, you may get a market rise and MACD turning down. Perhaps you think this is a sell signal. Well, it might not be a sell signal. Often in a strong market MACD will keep hovering in a high area, making little wiggles. It will flatten while the market is still going up." To avoid these kinds of false signals, Appel suggested not relying on any one indicator. "I would hate to put my life into any one single indicator," he commented.

To confirm a MACD bottom, Appel also looked at the New High–New Low indicator. "A diminution of new lows sometimes takes place even when the market averages are dropping," he said. "You begin to see more and more stocks holding support. That's a pretty good indication that some significant reversal is going to take place in the stock market."

The opposite occurs at market tops, Appel said. He explained: "As long as the number of issues making new highs keeps expanding, you're getting pretty good upside momentum. The number of new highs will decrease as the advance matures. The number of stocks participating and making new highs diminishes before the market averages turn down."

Appel said you want to use different parameters to help recognize a gradual shift in the market momentum: "If you are using MACD, I like to work with different time frames at the same time. Then all of the market events taking place begin to confirm together. But if you get a feeling the market is coming down and the short-term MACD begins to turn up, you want to see if it's a little blip or if you are getting changes in the intermediate MACD patterns. The more confidence you have, the better the chances you are going in the right direction."

Likewise, he said, as the market goes up and begins to turn, the shorter-term MACD begins to weaken first.

What MACD Does Best

Appel was remarkably humble about what MACD can do. "Basically, it gives you a picture of how market momentum is going," he said. "But there is a difference between price direction and momentum. In other words, if you're rising at a steep rate, you will see a lot of upside momentum. But suppose at some point, as it always does, the rise doesn't continue at that angle but continues at a lower angle. Perhaps MACD turns down but stock prices aren't turning down. In that case, it becomes an early signal."

For long-term market trends, Appel said the monthly MACD patterns give good confirming signals about two or three months after a major bear market bottom is over. "As long as you try not to get in on the first day," he noted, "it could tell you it's time to get into the market."

Can MACD be used to forecast market direction? "I don't use it as a forecaster as much as a guide or compass," Appel said. "As long as MACD is falling, I stay away. I don't know how long it's going to fall. And if it's rising, and you see a bullish-looking pattern, I stay with it until it turns down. When the indicator changes, we change. We don't try to guess when the indicator is going to reverse."

How to Use MACD

Appel suggested that people take the time to play with MACD to see how it works. He said: "We recommend that you maintain two or three MACD patterns at one time. Since the market drops faster than it rises, we usually recommend a quicker-reacting MACD pattern for a buy signal. You could use a 10-day over a 20-day or 25-day pattern. At tops they seem to be more gradual, so you should slow them down a little bit, so we might use a 20-day over a 40-day. These are given in exponential numbers, so it would be 0.11 over 0.22 for buying, and 0.15 and 0.075 for selling." These numbers should be viewed as rough guidelines.

Appel said that if you use a longer-term MACD, you can slow it down even more. He went on to say: "The question is whether you want to measure the intermediate or long term. If an intermediate term, you might use weekly patterns or just do it once a week. For short-term traders, you might want to use the daily MACD."

Traders at his firm typically use a top-down approach with MACD and other indicators to get a feel for the market. Then they will look at individual stocks they like that are trading well within that environment. Occasionally they'll use the hourly MACD for very short-term trading.

Indicators Don't Work Forever

At one time, Appel said, the fundamental indicator P/E (the price/earnings ratio) was an effective indicator. "When the market was over 20 P/E, that was considered a sign that stocks were too expensive and you had to be careful," he noted. "For decades people took this as the rule. But that went out the window in the 1990s. Stocks got up to 50 times earnings, and they stayed at higher levels."

He cautioned that people are always looking for something to latch onto. "If something works in the stock market twice in a row, people get excited. They want to believe it's magic."

His suggestion: "The best advice I can give someone is to devise and follow a plan. Don't expect the plan to be perfect. There should be room for phasing in and out. But operate with a plan because emotion will kill you. You want to try and make it as objective as possible. Never risk more than you can afford to lose because that will create bad decisions. And diversify among a lot of different things."

In the end, he said that you must admit you will be wrong, and not just a few times. "When you're wrong, take the loss. Don't let it build up, but try again the next time."

. . . .

Now that you understand MACD and the MACD histogram, in the next chapter you will be introduced to another extremely powerful oscillator, relative strength index (RSI). This alerts you when a stock or market is *overbought* or *oversold*. I believe you will find RSI intriguing.

CHAPTER 5

RSI

Welles Wilder introduced the relative strength index (RSI) to the world in 1978 by writing about it in an article for an engineering magazine. The RSI is a favorite of many traders because it gives early warning signals of *overbought* or *oversold* market conditions. Consider these signals as guidelines, not hard-and-fast rules. The goal is to gain an edge over other traders, and from my experience, RSI helps to give you that edge.

One reason that RSI is so popular is that it is one of the few *leading* indicators in technical analysis. In other words, it is forward-looking. On the other hand, MACD and moving averages, while extremely useful, are backward-looking (or lagging). They are not designed to forecast the future—only show you current or previous price action.

Although RSI cannot predict the future, it offers timely clues (but no magic answers). More importantly, it helps keep you out of trouble by alerting you to unsafe market conditions (overbought or oversold).

NOTE: RSI allows traders to observe "risk management" zones. If one of those zones or thresholds is broken, it's a red flag. While RSI is a very powerful oscillator, there is one thing it can't do with precision: time the market. Attempting to use RSI as a timing trigger will probably prove to be disappointing.

THE BASICS: HOW RSI WORKS

RSI is characterized as a "bounded" momentum oscillator that fluctuates between 0 and 100 with a default setting of 14 days. Although based on complicated formulas, it has only one signal line. When the RSI signal line rises above 70 and stays above, it's a signal that the market or stock is overbought. When RSI drops below 30 and stays below, it's a signal that the market or stock is oversold.

NOTE: *Overbought* is a technical term used to describe a security that has been subjected to continuous buying pressure and is due for a price correction. *Oversold* is a technical term used to describe a security that has been subjected to continuous selling pressure and is due for a price rebound.

RSI can be used in any time frame, but most traders prefer a daily or weekly period. In my experience, the weekly RSI gives the smoothest, less volatile signals. Day traders, however, should use the daily time period.

Although RSI warns of potential reversals, stocks can remain overbought or oversold for long time periods, one of the reasons you may not want to use RSI to time a reversal.

NOTE: Your charting software may have a list of RSI names such as *Slow RSI*, *Fast RSI*, *Full RSI* (a blend of fast and slow), and the original *RSI Wilder*. Most traders use RSI Wilder, which Welles Wilder created using the 14-day period and 70–30 readings.

RSI on a Chart

When you examine RSI on a stock chart, it typically appears at the top as a single line (this is the oscillator). If it doesn't appear automatically, select "RSI Wilder" from the drop-down menu.

Figure 5.1 is a screenshot of RSI on a stock chart. As you can see in this example, RSI was above 70, which means that the S&P 500 (SPX) was extremely overbought when this screenshot was taken. You can see that the odds of a reversal have increased, although no one would be able to say when it would occur (unsurprisingly, SPX reversed strongly a few days later).

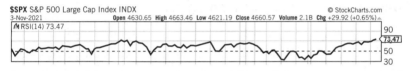

FIGURE 5.1 RSI
(Chart courtesy of StockCharts.com.)

RSI Problems and Limitations

Although RSI is a phenomenal tool, I don't want you to think it is perfect, because no indicator is flawless. For example, one of the challenges to RSI is that it can generate a lot of mixed signals, many that turn out to be false. Fortunately, using a weekly time period helps reduce the number of whipsaw-generating signals.

Another problem is that many traders mistakenly believe that as soon as RSI touches 70, it triggers an instantaneous sell signal; or if it tags 30, it is an instantaneous buy signal. That is not necessarily true. RSI has never made that claim (and if it could do that consistently, we'd all make a fortune).

It's recommended that you not get fixated on the 70 and 30 levels. Trader and author Alexander Elder explained it best when he wrote that oversold and overbought are like hot and cold readings on a thermometer. The same temperature has different meanings in summer and winter. Therefore, during bull markets or bear markets, these levels may adjust upward or downward.

More realistically, when the underlying stock rises above 70, it's a red flag. The stock is overbought even though it could keep trending higher. Risk-averse traders may feel uncomfortable holding an extremely overbought stock.

Another problem with RSI: Because it does not generate specific buy or sell signals, it is easy to get head-faked. To cut down on inaccurate results, use RSI in conjunction with other indicators.

NO VOLATILITY? WE HAVE A PROBLEM!

Oscillators such as RSI work best during volatile markets, with either the overall market or individual stocks. The main limitation of oscillators is that they don't perform as well during flat or sideways markets.

Another major problem with the effectiveness of oscillators has to do with computer algorithms (algos). These computer programs tend to neutralize some indicators, including RSI. That is one reason why stocks with an overbought reading of 70 RSI can keep moving higher and higher.

Basically, computer algos, based on their performance-chasing algorithms, can prevent some stocks from falling. How is this possible? Certain algos create buy programs that push stock prices higher, negating many standard technical signals. It is important that traders are aware of this limitation.

STATISTICALLY STUPID SIGNALS

As you already know, the maximum reading of RSI is 100, but if any stock is showing a reading of 80 or higher, for example, buying that stock presents risks that you don't need. Can the stock remain at elevated levels when RSI is ridiculously overbought? Yes, the stock can even go higher. I have seen some stocks have RSI readings of over 90.

When a stock moves so high that RSI is at the upper limits (over 95), traders will say that the stock is "burying the needle." This means that the stock is so overbought that RSI went right off the top of the scale.

Because RSI is a "bounded" oscillator, it is unable to go higher than 100, but at 98 or 99, it is at a dangerously extreme level. At either of these levels, it's questionable whether RSI is even working. Unfortunately, RSI will not tell you *when* a stock runs out of gas, only that the signal is "statistically stupid" and the stock should probably be avoided.

The good news is that these extremely high readings (98 and 99 RSI) are relatively rare, but when they do occur, you shouldn't expect them to be sustained for long. Of course there are exceptions: I have seen stocks that have remained overbought (over 70 to 80) for days, weeks, and months. Some stocks remain at overbought levels for so long that short sellers are forced to cover their losing positions based on margin call pressure. Nevertheless, the point of an indicator is to find valid signals, and RSI does that most of the time. Why fight the signals? The answer is, you shouldn't.

DON'T FIGHT THE TAPE

While it's not uncommon for stocks to stay overbought for long periods, it's rare for stocks to remain *oversold* for long. One theory is that retail investors, buy-the-dippers, those who invest in long-only funds, and algos are all trained to go long.

Therefore, when a stock is *oversold*, it's common for many market participants to buy the dip, trying to reverse the downturn. Obviously, this strategy cannot work every time, but it works more consistently than shorting the rip (shorting a rally).

Selling short *overbought* stocks is extra risky because when you are wrong, the stock can go higher by what feels like an infinite amount to anyone caught short. (Obviously, experienced short sellers, as well as the readers of this book, use stop losses to prevent their small losers from turning into big losers.)

If you are selling short stocks that are extremely overbought but keep going higher, forget the technical indicators and get out. As economist John Maynard Keynes once said, "The stock market can remain irrational longer than you can remain solvent." In other words, your risks increase if you bet against overbought or oversold stocks. Do so at your own peril.

In the stock market, sometimes stocks seem to be trading on a different planet, what I call trading in the "Twilight Zone." If you find yourself on the wrong side of *any* trade, don't fight the tape for very long.

THE BOTTOM LINE: Until we enter a lengthy bear market, the odds favor the bulls. Nevertheless, keep your eye on RSI for clues for when to take profits. Although it is difficult to time reversals, it never hurts to take a little money off the table when stocks enter into an overbought market environment.

TRADING TACTICS USING RSI

One thing you should know about overbought-oversold oscillators: Eventually stock prices hit a wall and reverse direction. That means that the stock price will rally when oversold, or fade when over-bought. It's a challenge to pin down the timing, although other indicators can help (consider learning about *stochastics* in Chapter 7, or try studying *Fibonacci* ratios, which often show stock prices retracing at 23.6 percent, 38.2 percent, 50 percent, and 61.8 percent).

One lesson I want to make clear: Indicators and oscillators offer guidance and clues but are not magic bullets. That's why it's important to have more than one piece of evidence before deciding what to trade.

> **NOTE:** Some traders look at too many indicators and have the opposite problem. More than four or five indicators on a chart is overkill for most traders. If using a dozen indicators or oscillators, for example, you are at risk of "analysis paralysis," a common trader ailment. With so many conflicting indicators, traders can't make up their mind about what to do, and end up doing nothing.

> **NOTE:** When using RSI or other indicators, be flexible (this is the "artistic" part of trading). Use these tools to get important clues, but making inflexible rules can backfire on you.

RSI Crossover Strategy

This strategy is used by many traders: After RSI rises above 70, they wait and watch. As soon as RSI falls back under 70, they *sell short* (or sell if they already own the stock). Conversely, if RSI falls under 30, traders may wait. As soon as RSI rises back above 30, they feel it's a green light to *buy* the stock.

Although this strategy is not for everyone, there is a large group of traders who use it. This simple strategy is very easy to test, so I recommend doing so in a simulated trading program.

Bearish and Bullish Divergences

A clever way of using RSI is to look for divergences between RSI and the underlying stock. For example, when a stock is moving higher but RSI is moving lower (i.e., *bearish divergence*), RSI is giving you a clue that the stock may be on borrowed time. In other words, the rising stock price may be a head fake or a "false positive."

On the other hand, when a stock is moving lower but RSI is moving higher, that is considered a *bullish divergence*. Here's a more detailed explanation of divergences.

- **Bearish divergence.** When YYYY is moving higher but RSI is moving lower, not only is that a bearish divergence, but it could be a *bull trap*. The bulls believe YYYY is unstoppable, but RSI is telling a different story. As you may remember, momentum always reverses before the trend. It's "possible" that the underlying stock will reverse in this example, but once again—confirm with other indicators before making the trade.

- **Bullish divergence.** Let's say that ZYX is moving lower but RSI is climbing higher. This not only is a bullish divergence but is also known as a *bear trap*. Inexperienced bearish traders might chase ZYX lower while ignoring the stronger RSI signal. In this example, RSI is telling us that momentum is building so the drop in the stock may be a head fake. In fact, in this example, ZYX reverses direction and rips higher, trapping the bears, who ignored the bullish divergence signal.

NOTE: Divergences don't work 100 percent of the time, so don't commit a large amount of capital if you see this signal on a chart.

Other RSI Signals

Although the default settings of a 14-day time period and 70-30 overbought-oversold parameters work for most people, feel free to try other time periods to find what works for you. For example, you could use 75 and 25 rather than 70 and 30. Some short-term traders change the 14-day time period to a 6-day or 9-day period. A position trader might change it to a 25-day period. Any changes that are made impact the signal, so test before trading once the defaults have changed.

The 70-30 default settings are guidelines and are not permanent. Nevertheless, they have been backtested by many traders, and based on studies and research, the default parameters have stood the test of time. Until you gain more experience with RSI indicators, stick with the default settings.

When RSI Is Neutral

Here's a fact that many traders don't know: When RSI or any other "bounded" oscillators near the 50 percent level, it is a neutral reading. If RSI is resting on its 50 percent indicator level, it means that after 14 trading days, the stock is neither overbought nor oversold. This is neither a strong buy nor a sell signal. Waiting for RSI to cross 70 or 30 is far more reliable than trading in the middle.

THE VIX

One of the best ways to measure investor fear and greed is to use the VIX (Chicago Board Options Exchange Volatility Index). I covered the VIX in my previous book, but this topic is so important that I feel obligated to do a more detailed review.

This popular sentiment indicator is widely believed to measure the mood of the market. Nicknamed the "fear index," it helps traders assess how much fear is in the marketplace.

The VIX is an estimate of the future volatility of the US stock market. Although the math is complicated, the VIX gives useful insights into how volatile the markets will be over the near term (according to option traders). It's often used as a contrarian indicator. (A popular saying is "When the VIX is low, it's time to go. When the VIX is high, it's time to buy.")

> **ADVANCED NOTE:** The VIX is calculated using a formula that averages the weighted prices of out-of-the-money puts and calls that expire in 16 to 44 days. By using real-world option prices, the VIX measures how all option traders in total are estimating future market volatility for the next 30 days.

When the VIX Is Low

As implied volatility decreases, the VIX declines (by definition). For example, when the VIX is low (under 15), it reflects extreme complacency among option traders. The market tends to be calm, and there is little fear of a market decline among these traders. It's important to note that the VIX can remain low for long periods before eventually moving higher.

When the VIX Is High

When the VIX moves sharply higher (above 30 or 40), it reflects excessive buying of put options, and that means that fear is rampant among option traders. As implied volatility increases, the VIX rises. A VIX spike occurs primarily because nervous traders rush to buy put options. These traders need puts to hedge their portfolios, or seek to profit from the downturn they believe is coming. That increased demand causes the prices of both calls and puts to rise, and that results in an increase in implied volatility for all options.

Fearful traders buy puts, and lots of them. They are not afraid of a rally and are not interested in buying call options. The increased demand for puts results in a rising VIX.

The rising VIX is a signal that a short-term bottom, or an oversold condition in the stock market, is likely, but not until the excessive demand for put options abates. Generally, when the VIX surpasses a 40 reading, there has been panic buying of put options (for protection and speculation). In times of extreme volatility, the VIX may move to levels above 50.

The fear and panic, however, typically does not last long. When the VIX reaches levels of that magnitude, fear of an outright crash is widespread and may signify a severe market correction. For contrarians who have an opposite mindset from the crowd, it is a buying opportunity.

NOTE: For the record, the VIX printed a high above 86 on March 20, 2020, during the height of the Covid-19 pandemic. In hindsight, it was one of the greatest buying opportunities in history. From the March lows, the stock market rose to all-time highs in 2021. (Option experts tell me that if the VIX had existed during the 1987 crash, it would have reached levels near 150.)

NOTE: The VIX is displayed on your brokerage firm's website and on numerous financial websites. It is an optionable security, meaning you can trade puts and calls on the VIX itself.

. . . .

Now that you have a more thorough understanding of RSI (and the VIX), and what it can do for you, it's time to introduce one of the most popular technical oscillators in technical analysis: Bollinger Bands.

Because so many traders use Bollinger Bands, we will have a robust discussion on how to use this tool to improve your trading results.

CHAPTER 6

BOLLINGER BANDS

ollinger Bands, developed by John Bollinger, are one of the most popular indicators in technical analysis, a reason they're part of nearly every charting program. Among other things, this flexible indicator helps to identify whether a stock or market is overbought or oversold, how a stock or market is trending, and the degree of volatility in that trend.

While Bollinger Bands provide very useful information, many traders use this indicator without understanding all its features. In this chapter, I hope to clear up some of the confusion.

Bollinger Bands can be viewed with any time frame depending on the trader's preference. Bollinger Bands are commonly used with a daily price chart but are just as effective with the weekly or monthly chart. In addition, many short-term traders use Bollinger Bands with intraday charts.

THE BASICS

Bollinger Bands consist of two components. First, there is an upper band and lower band, displayed in blue or black. The dotted line between the bands represents the 20-day simple moving average, a key part of the Bollinger Band methodology.

Many traders don't realize that the 20-day moving average line is a key ingredient of Bollinger Bands. After all, the term *moving average* is used because Bollinger Bands are calculated by using the average of the most recent 20 days of the ever-changing stock price.

Those two bands were purposely designed to be set two *standard deviations* away from the 20-day moving average line (an expanded discussion of standard deviation comes later in this chapter). For a stock (or the market) to pierce the upper or lower band, it must make a strong move.

> **NOTE:** The default values for Bollinger Bands are 20 days and two standard deviations. Some short-term traders may change the 20-day moving average default to a 10-day moving average. In addition, Bollinger Bands can and should be used to confirm signals from some of your other favorite indicators.

Here are two of the most basic Bollinger Band signals:

1. **Overbought.** When the stock price pierces (crosses) the upper band, the security is in overbought territory.
2. **Oversold.** When the stock price pierces (crosses) the lower band, the security is in oversold territory.

Remember that just because a stock is overbought or oversold doesn't mean that a reversal is imminent.

Bollinger Bands were designed to help a trader with the following two concepts:

1. Whether the price of the underlying asset is relatively high (overbought) or relatively low (oversold)
2. Whether the volatility of the stock price is trending higher or lower

When using Bollinger Bands, there are two important rules that traders must follow: First, the bands must be used in pairs (both the upper and the lower band), and second, the bands must be combined with a moving average and never used separately.

Figure 6.1 shows how Bollinger Bands look on a chart. Because Bollinger Bands are displayed on top of the stock chart, the four lines can confuse some traders. After a few practice sessions, they are easier to interpret.

FIGURE 6.1   Bollinger Bands
(Chart courtesy of BollingerBands.us.)

NOTE: In Figure 6.1, notice how the stock price (displayed as a candlestick) bounces between the upper and lower bands and how it moves above and below the 20-day moving average.

NOTE: Bollinger Bands are a type of *price envelope*, defined as a graph consisting of two price ranges: upper and lower.

How Bollinger Bands Use Standard Deviation

As you can see in Figure 6.1, Bollinger Bands are constructed by combining three different plots on a single chart. First is the simple 20-day moving average of the underlying asset's closing price. Next, two additional plots are added.

These lines represent a price that is two *standard deviations* above the moving average (upper band) and two *standard deviations* below the moving average (lower band). By definition, the moving average is always halfway between the upper and lower bands.

The *standard deviation* is a key ingredient of the Bollinger Bands method. Standard deviation is used in statistics to measure the consistency of a set of data points, but more importantly for our purposes, as a way to measure risk.

Two standard deviations represent a stock price change that's outside the norm, and occurs about 1 day in every 20 days. Therefore, when a stock tags or pierces through either of the bands, it's a warning sign that a stock or index is overbought or oversold.

This is how Bollinger Bands work, and it's important: The moving average tends to bounce between the upper and lower bands. The moving average bends, turns, and moves independently of the bands.

> **NOTE:** The dotted line describes the change in the stock price, while the bands describe the stock's recent volatility. The bands offer a glimpse into potential price action based on the stock's volatility. As the stock becomes more volatile, the bands move apart, signifying the possibility of larger daily price changes.

Watch the Bands!

Here's a fact: When using the default settings, 95 percent of the time the stock price will remain within the upper and lower bands. Only 5 percent of the time will it move beyond one of the two bands.

How is this information important? It makes sense to trade based on what happens to the stock price 95 percent of the time. However, here's a big caveat: It's mandatory to prevent your position from getting hammered when one of those "not so rare" events occurs (a price change in the wrong direction that exceeds two standard deviations).

The good news is that a stock price moves in a winning direction during half of those 5 percent occurrences (when the stock price goes outside the bands). Therefore, be ready to capitalize when the opportunity arises.

ADVANCED NOTE: If you change the default to *one* standard deviation (rather than two), that 95 percent number above changes to 68 percent. Change the default to *three* standard deviations, and 99.7 percent of the time, the price remains between the two bands. As rare as 3 chances in 1,000 may seem, three standard deviation price moves do occur about once every four years. Betting against them sends some traders to the poorhouse.

ADVANCED HINT: John Bollinger suggested that experienced traders may change the default settings. Instead of using the defaults of 20 and 2, his idea was to try a 50-period moving average and a 2.1 standard deviation. For an even longer-term perspective, change the default setting to 20 weeks and use a weekly time period.

Walking the Bands

As you already know from RSI, stocks can remain overbought or oversold for a long time before reversing. Therefore, these are not actionable buy or sell signals. In fact, if you observe Bollinger Bands long enough, you'll notice that the stock may linger along the upper or lower band for quite some time.

Some traders get impatient when the stock "walks the bands." Sometimes a stock can remain wrapped around one of the bands for days. At other times, after reaching the band, it may immediately reverse and head toward the moving average.

Support and Resistance

The upper and lower bands may serve as support and resistance for individual stocks. When prices approach or touch the upper band, the stock is said to be testing resistance. When prices approach or touch the lower band, the stock is said to be testing support. If a stock breaks below support, it could signal the start of a downtrend. And if the stock breaks out above resistance, it could signal the start of an upward trend.

Understanding Volatility

Bollinger Bands also help traders think about and analyze volatility. The bands drawn by the software represent a gauge of how quickly, and by how much, the stock price has the potential to change.

Stocks that are more volatile have larger daily price swings than do stocks with lesser volatility. Therefore, when volatility is high, traders should anticipate that high volatility (resulting in larger than average daily price changes) will continue over the very short term.

Bollinger Bands measure volatility, widening during volatile periods and contracting during less volatile periods. For example, if the upper and lower bands suddenly contract (squeeze together), it's because the stock has been less volatile.

Don't be fooled by a low-volatility environment. When Bollinger Bands are extremely narrow, it is a sign that the market may suddenly move in the opposite direction. Put another way, periods of low volatility are often followed by periods of high volatility.

The unknown factor is how much time must pass before the change happens. It's probably the wrong move to take a position in anticipation of a volatility breakout. Periods of low volatility (complacency) can last for years.

It works the other way too. If the bands are expanding, it means that the price of the underlying stock has been volatile. The expanding Bollinger Bands could result in the market reversing direction. The market tends not to remain highly volatile for too long, but the results can be dramatic (October 1987 and the years 2007 to 2009 are good examples of this phenomenon).

To make the best use of Bollinger Bands, keep your eye on how the bands are *expanding* and *contracting* (a measure of volatility). Many traders overlook this key feature of Bollinger Bands because they focus too much on prices rather than the bands.

Let's expand this conversation right now (no pun intended).

Expand and Contract

Understanding how the bands expand and contract (diverge or converge) is what sets this indicator apart from most others. As you just read, when the bands move apart, volatility and momentum are increasing. When the bands tighten, volatility and momentum are decreasing. Pay attention to how the bands expand because it is a warning sign that risks have increased.

When prices fall, the bands are expanding and volatility is usually increasing as downside selling pressure accelerates. If volatility is increasing as the stock price falls, don't buy no matter how oversold the stock may be. Buying into a long position in this scenario can lead to a world of pain.

Instead, wait until volatility stops increasing and subsides and for the trend to turn. At that point, buying becomes less risky. It takes patience to wait, but it's one of the key characteristics of successful traders.

> **REMINDER:** One of the reasons many traders get caught on the wrong side of a trend is that they aren't reading the bands correctly. For example, the stock price may be rising while the bands are contracting.

> **NOTE:** Be sure to watch the *slope* of the band and follow its direction (for example, whether it turns up or down). Studying the slope of the Bollinger Band—whether it is descending, ascending, or flat—allows you to see the full picture.

HOW TRADERS MISUSE BOLLINGER BANDS

The 20-day moving average gives an idea of the trend: up, down, or sideways. Traders often misuse this indicator by using a move through the dotted moving average line as a buy or sell trigger (the popular *crossover* signal).

In fact, when traders mistakenly make a buy or sell decision based on a Bollinger Band crossover, some blame Bollinger Bands for poor trading results. In reality, the Achilles' heel of Bollinger Bands is that they weren't designed to give precise buy and sell signals.

Another common mistake made by Bollinger Band users occurs when they see the stock price fall and perhaps tag the lower band. They assume the stock will reverse direction and move higher. In fact, a tag of the lower band does *not* mean that the stock will reverse direction and move higher.

Conversely, just because the stock price tags the upper band doesn't mean it will suddenly reverse direction and move lower. No one knows where the stock price is headed after it tags a band. The bottom line: A tag is not a trade signal for Bollinger Band users.

NOTE: If you are new to Bollinger Bands, all these guidelines may seem confusing. If your head is spinning, go to the sidebar "Interview with John Bollinger" at the end of this chapter; I believe that after you read it, this indicator will make a lot more sense.

Few traders use Bollinger Bands to their full potential. Nevertheless, many traders use the most basic Bollinger Band signals successfully, and you can too. It's a great place to start.

NOTE: One of the best ways to use Bollinger Bands is not as a forecasting tool but as a risk management tool (credit to Professor Jeffrey Bierman, CMT, for articulating how to use Bollinger Bands in this way).

ADDITIONAL BOLLINGER BAND OBSERVATIONS

If you do use this indicator, take the time to review the following key observations about Bollinger Bands, which will help you understand them better:

- When volatility has increased, the bands separate. When that separation is especially large, any existing trend may be on the verge of ending.
- The stock price can wrap itself around one of the bands for a long time when a trend is strong (called *walking the bands*). When a momentum oscillator suggests that it's time to exit the trade, consider taking profits or reducing position size.
- The stock price tends to bounce, touching one of the bands and then the other. These swings can be used by a trader to select profit targets. For example, after the stock price touches and then moves away from the lower band, if it

crosses the moving average, the upper band becomes a tradable target.

• When volatility is low and the bands tighten, the chances increase that a rapid price move (in either direction) will occur. If that move is a new trend, the profit potential is significant. Always be alert to the possibility of a false move in the opposite direction.

Now that you have a deeper understanding of this fascinating indicator, I have a special treat. The creator of Bollinger Bands, John Bollinger, spoke with me a few years ago about some of the creative ways he uses Bollinger Bands.

INTERVIEW WITH JOHN BOLLINGER

Using a first-generation desktop computer in the 1980s, John Bollinger was an option trader who wanted to test whether volatility was a fixed number, the prevalent belief at the time. He was concerned with how options were priced, which was primarily based on knowing volatility. "In those days," he said, "we believed that volatility was a fixed number and didn't change. We thought it was part of the property of a security."

That changed when he copied the volatility formula into a spreadsheet. "For the first time I saw that volatility was not fixed but was actually a dynamic number," he explains. "It was changing all the time. And I said, 'That's interesting!'" Over the course of the next few months, with trial and error and different forms of volatility calculations, he came up with Bollinger Bands.

The creative ways that people, especially option traders, use his indicator has amazed Bollinger. "People reported using it in ways that I never imagined," he marvels. "I received some tremendously good ideas from people who called in and said, 'Guess what I'm doing with the Bollinger Bands?' And I reply, 'Oh really? I hadn't thought of that one yet!'"

One of the reasons that Bollinger Bands have remained popular is that they easily adapt to market conditions, he says. He goes on to say: "The components of Bollinger Bands are trend and volatility. These are essential market forces. And they are depicted in a manner that is intuitively easy for people to grasp."

The Proper Use of Bollinger Bands

Bollinger explains what his indicator actually does: "Bollinger Bands primarily tell you whether prices are high or low on a relative basis. Their best usage is to generate trading setups that can be used to calculate the probability of a successful trade. When you find one of these high-probability trades, act on it."

What Bollinger Bands cannot do, he cautions, is to provide continuous advice: "Can you look at any given point in time at Bollinger Bands and know what to do? The answer, at least in my practice, is no."

He says that Bollinger Bands are not forecasting tools. They can't predict how the Dow Jones Industrial Average will perform on any given day. Nevertheless, he acknowledges that within the Bollinger Band setups "there are obvious targets and obvious projections that can be made. It's especially useful to see whether or not a setup is working. But I wouldn't call that market forecasting."

One phenomenon unique to Bollinger Bands is that stocks tend to stay overbought or oversold for extended time periods. "We call that a walk up the bands," he explains, "or a walk down the bands. It's perfectly normal. In fact, that's the sort of activity to be expected in a trending market. It may take a long time to find a usable setup."

If someone gets impatient because there's no immediate buy or sell signal, he suggests that the person, not the tool, has failed.

He adds: "The biggest mistake that people make with my indicator is to assume that any tag of the upper band is an automatic sell, and that any tag of the lower band is an automatic buy. That's completely wrong."

Another problem is that people get fixated on certain signals even though the market is pushing against them. As a result, they go through a lot of pain. The key, Bollinger says, is to be flexible. Think of these trading bands as a component of a system analysis that also includes trend and sentiment information. He notes, "It's more useful to think of my trading bands as part of a whole trading system rather than being the only tool needed."

Experiment

In Bollinger's opinion, the best way to use his indicator is to experiment with the defaults. "Fool around with the defaults as widely and creatively as possible," he suggests.

"Eventually you could find that sweet spot that works really well for you. One way to find it is by changing the moving averages from simple to exponential to weighted, or change the number of periods, or the number of bands. Then try it on a 10-minute, daily, hourly, weekly, and monthly chart."

Avoid a Stale Trading System

Although Bollinger created a series of hard-and-fast rules for using his indicator, he discovered they didn't work out as well as he expected. "The markets morph and change over time. While one particular set of rules may work in one period, they may fail to work or even work in a contrary manner during another period," he says. "I found that the real value is to make my approach as adaptive as possible, so they morph with the markets. This prevents you from getting caught with a stale trading system, one that is no longer viable for the market."

NOTE: Bollinger wrote a book about his indicator, *Bollinger on Bollinger Bands* (McGraw Hill).

. . . .

Many beginner traders want to know if there is an indicator that gives real-time alerts of reversals or overbought and oversold conditions. If there were such an indicator, it would help with market timing. In fact, there is such an indicator: *stochastics.*

Many consider stochastics as one of the most powerful indicators in technical analysis. It does everything mentioned above and more. This next chapter is a discussion you shouldn't miss.

CHAPTER 7

STOCHASTICS

The stochastic oscillator (stochastics) is a favorite tool of many short- and long-term traders because it provides reliable and surprisingly accurate buy and sell signals. It is both powerful and versatile, one of the reasons that many traders display it on their screen at all times.

This indicator has multiple uses besides offering trade signals: First, it warns of overbought and oversold conditions. Second, it alerts traders to potential reversals. Finally, it confirms whether the reversal has actually taken place. For all these reasons, using stochastics should improve your trading. (I will go into the details later in this chapter.)

Ralph Dystant, a Chicago dentist who also ran a technical analysis educators' group, was reportedly the first to create the stochastic oscillator. After Dystant's untimely death, his teaching assistant, George Lane, continued to make improvements to the stochastics formula. Lane also wrote numerous articles on how to use it, making the oscillator even more popular. Tim Slater, who belonged to a group that helped to develop numerous indicators in the 1970s, was the first to coin the name, *stochastics*.

If you have never used stochastics or believe that it is too complex, you're missing out on a multidimensional indicator that can improve your trading results. You may have heard that "no one can time the market." Contrary to that saying, when stochastics is used properly, it's possible to time your entries and exits. That's another reason why it's worthwhile to learn this fascinating oscillator.

THE IDEA BEHIND STOCHASTICS

If you are new to stochastics, it may seem confusing at first. However, when you use stochastics on a chart, the signals are remarkably easy to interpret. I'll also do my best to make it understandable. My hope is, by the time you finish this chapter, you should have enough information to start using stochastics immediately.

There are many misconceptions about how stochastics works, so you may find surprises in this chapter. For example, many people don't realize that stochastics is both a *momentum* indicator and a *trend* indicator. That makes stochastics a very powerful tool because it allows users to get in and out of positions in a timely manner.

The basic idea behind stochastics is that the momentum of a stock price frequently changes before the stock price changes direction. Therefore, stochastics can be used to predict trend reversals.

WHAT IS STOCHASTICS?

Here is a definition to consider: Stochastics shows the closing price of an asset (a stock, etc.) and compares that closing price with where that stock has been trading (the high and low range) over the past 14 days.

By using stochastics, you can identify changes in momentum and trend, spot overbought and oversold conditions, and receive actionable buy and sell signals.

The Basics

On most charting packages, multiple stochastic names appear in a drop-down list. The two main programs are *Slow Stochastics* and *Fast Stochastics*. Intraday traders tend to use Fast Stochastics because it generates more signals and at a faster pace (there is less lag).

On the other hand, the advantage of using Slow Stochastics is that it reduces the number of "whipsaws." It is not better or worse than Fast Stochastics, but it generates fewer trade signals and fewer false crossovers.

Ultimately, it's your choice which version to use, but if you are a beginner, I'd recommend starting with Slow Stochastics.

> **HINT:** Stochastics works well in all kinds of market environments, while indicators such as moving averages, MACD, and RSI were designed to do better in trending markets. When a stock or the overall market is moving sideways or, worse, randomly moving up and down in a range, stochastics should help recognize when that pattern may be ending.

%D and %K

Stochastics is displayed as two lines, %D (the slower line) and %K (the faster line).

> **IMPORTANT:** %K changes more rapidly than %D.

Since it's easier to explain %D and %K visually, Figure 7.1 is what Slow Stochastics looks like on a stock chart (look at the top of the chart). The faster %K line is in black. The slower %D line is in red (it's gray in this book).

A number of actionable signals appear on stochastics. For now, I'll show you the most basic signals.

FIGURE 7.1 Slow Stochastics
(Chart courtesy of Stockcharts.com.)

ACTIONABLE SIGNAL: When the two lines (%K and %D) *cross* while the indicator is overbought or oversold, that constitutes a buy or sell signal. To be specific, when %K crosses %D, that's an actionable buy or sell signal as long as the stochastics is above 80 or below 20. You can read more about these signals in the "80-20 Crossover Strategy" section of this chapter.

Remember, %K is the *leader* line. Because %D is a smoother version of %K, it is slower. The way these two lines converge and diverge is what makes stochastics so beneficial and one of the most amazing discoveries in technical analysis.

ADVANCED NOTE: The %K line subtracts the lowest low from the highest high over the last 14 days to define a price range. Next, it displays the last closing price as a percentage of this range. The %D line is a three-day moving average of %K. Because %D is a moving average, it changes more slowly than %K.

As the stock price changes, the %K and %D lines illustrate the changing momentum. To use an analogy, pretend that you're driving a car. As you let your foot off the gas, the car's momentum decreases even though the car is still moving forward. It's the same with %K and %D.

(14) and (3) Periods

In addition to %K and %D, there are two default numbers in parentheses written as (14,3). If you look closely at the upper left of Figure 7.1, you'll see that the numbers are displayed like this: %K (14) %D (3). This means that %K uses the last 14 periods (typically days), while %D is a 3-day simple moving average of %K. It's plotted alongside %K to act as a signal or trigger line. A period can be measured in hours, days, weeks, or months depending on the time frame of the trader.

When George Lane developed stochastics, he chose 14 as the default period. However, some short-term traders believe that %K (14) is too slow for them, one reason why some charting programs use (10) as the default period. Some intraday traders went further and lowered it to (5). That's a fast signal suited mostly for day traders. Feel free to change the defaults to any numbers that suit your needs, but I recommend beginning by using the chart defaults.

HINT: In an extremely low-volatility environment, some traders increase the %K speed just so they can find an actionable trade. The danger, however, is that a faster %K leads to a greater probability of receiving false signals. It's not wise to force a signal just to find a trade.

0 and 100

Another feature of stochastics is that the minimum reading is 0 and the maximum reading is 100. Put another way, it is *bounded* from 0 to 100 (similar to RSI). When above 80, a stock (or index) is considered to be overbought. Below 20, a stock (or index) is considered to be oversold.

As you learned in previous chapters, overbought and oversold are a *condition*, not an actionable trade or trigger. Don't make the common mistake of blindly buying a stock when it drops below 20 or selling short (or selling an existing position) when it rises above 80. It's true that on occasion this strategy may work for you, but it was not how stochastics was designed to function.

WHAT IS MEANT BY OVERBOUGHT AND OVERSOLD?

To understand oscillators, you must understand that *overbought* and *oversold* are relative terms that depend on market conditions. As you know from reading about RSI, both stocks and indexes can remain overbought or oversold for extended time periods. In addition, 80 and 20 are guidelines, not rules, and can be adjusted upward or downward as market conditions change.

Taking an immediate position is the mistake that many rookie traders make because they don't fully understand how stochastics works. Contrarian beginners tend to jump into a trade, taking a short position when they observe an overbought signal, but are shocked when the stock gets even more overbought.

Conversely, when a stock is oversold and is below 20 on stochastics, it doesn't mean it will immediately rally. Although it's due for a bounce and may reverse in the future, it isn't the right time to buy the dip immediately. It's more like a red flag. Stochastics is signaling that the stock is oversold and could reverse direction in an extreme way. If you are short and have a decent profit, it would be wise to take your profits because a reversal is likely.

In the real trading world, no one can tell you exactly when the reversal may occur. Nevertheless, no technical indicator gives better clues than stochastics.

When Stocks Are Chronically Overbought or Oversold

One of the biggest problems with stochastics is that some stocks (or some indexes) move so high that they become chronically overbought. If a stock remains at a "statistically stupid" price level for a protracted time period, it may be time to abandon the trade and look for better candidates. At ridiculously high prices, it's likely that stochastics and other oscillators have lost their edge, one of the limitations of oscillators like stochastics and RSI.

The same problem can occur with chronically oversold stocks. However, the odds are often a little better that buyers will step in and bring an extremely oversold stock higher. The only time buyers may *not* step in is during a bear market or when a stock is so damaged that buyers stay away.

WHAT STOCHASTICS DOES BEST

The theory behind stochastics is that in an uptrend, prices will close near the high of the day's trading range, and in a downtrend, prices will close near the low. However, prices often get too overextended and overbought, or are sold too heavily by investors and become oversold.

When that happens, you can use stochastics to identify extremes. As mentioned earlier, even though the levels are set at 80 and 20 to denote overbought and oversold, both terms are "relative," meaning they are not precisely defined.

With that in mind, stochastics lets you know when extreme levels are reached (over 80 and under 20). More importantly, it can issue alerts or warnings that tell you when a stock is near the top, bottom, or middle of a range. This gives you important information but also provides you the flexibility to decide which trades to make with this data.

USE STOCHASTICS TO TRACK MOMENTUM

If you look at %K and %D on a chart and see they are falling, it simply means that momentum is slowing for that individual stock. It does not mean the stock is going to plunge. Perhaps the stock ran up too high and too fast and is exhausted; stochastics gives clues to when that momentum weakens.

Put another way, stochastics is used to track momentum and not only the trend. Think of stochastics as a speedometer: It helps to evaluate the strength of the momentum. Unlike other popular indicators, stochastics does not follow the stock price or volume. Instead, it gives you an idea of how fast or slow a stock is moving (momentum).

How is this important? Remember what I wrote earlier: Momentum changes direction before price. This is key; by studying stochastics on a stock chart, you get clues to when momentum changes direction. If stochastics works as intended, price will follow.

For example, while other traders are still following the stock price as it moves higher, and perhaps adding to their position, stochastics may alert you that momentum has slowed, and perhaps even reversed direction (%K will reverse first because it's faster. When %K crosses %D and the stochastics is above 80 or below 20, that's a true, actionable signal).

If the signal is correct and you interpreted it correctly, you can close your position *before* the stock price reverses direction. One major benefit of stochastics is to anticipate reversals. That is why it is so popular with traders who have taken the time to learn it.

NOTE: It is fascinating to watch %K and %D converge, diverge, and intersect. Be aware of the difference between the two lines *converging* (approaching one another) versus *crossing* (intersecting with one another).

As you will learn next, when the two lines cross while in over-bought or oversold territory, that gives a much stronger signal.

THE 80-20 CROSSOVER STRATEGY

Many rookies have been told to sell stocks short or sell existing stock positions as soon as %K and %D move above 80. They have also been told to go long when %K and %D drop below 20. This is a popular strategy, and if it works for you, keep doing what works.

On the other hand, based on research and studies, here are two tradable signals that are unknown by many traders:

1. When stochastics rises above 80 and there is a crossover (%K line crosses %D line), that is a signal to short (or sell existing long positions). There must be a crossover above 80 for a signal to be generated.
2. When stochastics falls below 20 and there is a crossover, that is a signal to go long. There must be a crossover below 20 for a signal to be generated.

Some traders change the thresholds to 70 and 30 to generate more signals, but it's a personal choice whether to use 80-20 or 70-30. You may miss a lot of trade opportunities using 80-20.

Looking for crossovers in the middle is not recommended because those signals are not as reliable. While I know that many traders look for crossover signals in the middle, and it may work for some, the above criteria generate significant signals.

NOTE: Although these signals are significant, they are only guidelines that are not set in stone.

NOTE: Many experienced traders wait for stochastics to move outside the range (80-20 or 70-30) and then wait for the crossover before buying or selling.

A CAVEAT: If you are a momentum trader who wants to squeeze every last penny out of a strong uptrend, you may purposely ride the stock higher and ignore the crossover. Just be aware that if %K reverses, it tends to be an early warning sign that the stock price may soon follow. If you're not paying attention, it's easy to get caught on the losing side.

NOT A PERFECT OSCILLATOR

I wish I could tell you that the secret sauce in technical analysis is stochastics—but it's not. When using this indicator, it's possible to be too early or too late. In fact, you should expect it to happen intermittently. This is one reason to use Slow Stochastics, because its smoothing factor reduces the frequency of false signals.

Obviously, some impatient traders may immediately trade based on the actions of the faster %K. Sure, trading on those signals may work, but probably not often enough. Often, %D won't cross %K, and the sell signal won't be confirmed. I can't tell you how to trade, but it's often a mistake to react too quickly to the signals. Sometimes a little patience is required.

NOTE: Accept the fact that you are going to miss some trades with stochastics because you may not react quickly enough.

SLOW VERSUS FAST VERSUS FULL

Let's briefly discuss the various versions of stochastics. The three main types are slow, fast, and *full*. As mentioned earlier, Slow Stochastics is just what it says: slower. It is designed to generate lagging signals because it incorporates a moving average. It's ideal for swing or position traders or short-term investors who want fewer but more significant triggers.

Fast Stochastics is more price sensitive and therefore generates more signals. George Lane and his colleagues created Fast Stochastics before they created Slow Stochastics. When side by side on a chart, you can see the difference in how they react. More signals also mean more potential head fakes. That's why I often remind you to confirm with other indicators before buying or selling. Stochastics, while a brilliant indicator, is not perfect. Use a suite of indicators if you want the most reliable information.

Full Stochastics confuses many people because it's nearly identical to Slow Stochastics. What's so special about Full Stochastics? The answer is that you can customize the number of periods for %K and %D. Full Stochastics is good for experienced traders who want to alter the variables. Slow Stochastics, on the other hand, has a fixed number of smoothing periods and can't be customized.

Some traders ask, "Which one is better? Slow or Fast?" It's not about which is better, because both are excellent. The answer is to adjust the defaults so that the signals generated by stochastics fit your trading style and strategies. Slow Stochastics gives fewer signals, while Fast Stochastics reacts faster to changes in momentum. Both are good at catching stock rotations.

HINT: Test stochastics in a simulated trading program to see whether it generates actionable signals.

ADVANCED STOCHASTICS ANALYSIS

For those who want to dig even deeper into stochastics, the stock chart (and analysis) shown in Figure 7.2 should meet your needs.

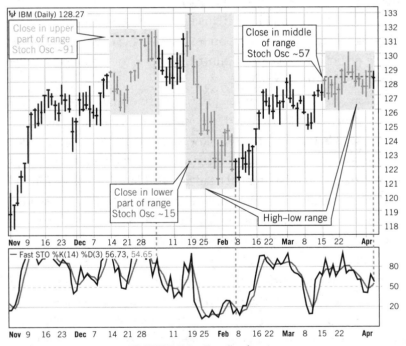

FIGURE 7.2 Fast Stochastics
(Chart courtesy of StockCharts.com.)

Figure 7.2 shows when the underlying asset is overbought (above 80) or oversold (below 20). In either circumstance, the stock is poised to reverse direction, although the timing is unknown.

Trend Changes

The chart in Figure 7.2 also displays the daily price range (vertical line) with the most recent closing price (horizontal line). One stochastic concept is that when a stock is in an uptrend, the closing price tends to be near the daily high, and when a stock is in a downtrend, the closing price tends to be near the daily low. When that no longer occurs, it's a warning that the trend may be coming to an end.

Digging Deeper

In Figure 7.2, you can see that the stochastic oscillator is 91 (that value appears in the box in the upper left corner of the chart), which is significantly above 80 and well into overbought territory.

The chart also shows that the closing prices have been at the upper end of the daily range. Notice that the stock price dipped before one final rally to $133. During that rally, the closing prices weren't always near the day's high and in fact were often in the bottom half. That was a warning of a trend reversal. Sure enough, a serious decline to less than $122 followed.

At that price, the stochastic oscillator was 15 (see the box at the center bottom of the chart), and the stock was seriously oversold. As the stock rose to ~$124, the closing price moved near the day's high, warning of an end to the downtrend. The stock quickly rallied to ~$127 as the closing highs moved to midrange.

Trade Signals

Unlike most indicators, stochastics gives actionable, reliable signals. For a trade signal to occur, first, the asset must be overbought or oversold. Second, the faster %K line must cross over the slower %D line.

When both conditions are met, the signals are the most reliable. It may be tempting to act on a signal when the stochastics reading is 78 or 79 (or 21 or 22), but that violates the rules. It may seem like a good idea to anticipate that the lines will cross within a day or two, but it's wise not to do that. It pays to have patience and wait for a true, viable signal.

Again, in Figure 7.2, look at the stochastics chart (bottom of the chart). On February 9, the %K (black) line crossed the %D (red line or gray in a book) when the stochastic oscillator was 15. That's a true buy signal. As soon as %K crossed above %D while oversold, the stock moved substantially higher.

NOTE: The steps in calculating the stochastic oscillator are given in the Indicator Glossary near the end of this book.

. . . .

Now that you know a lot more about stochastics, I'd like to introduce you to one of the most popular stock charts in technical analysis: *candlesticks*. Many traders rely on candlesticks to read the overall market and use its patterns to trade stocks. I think you'll enjoy the next chapter.

CHAPTER 8

CANDLESTICKS

C andlesticks are the oldest form of technical analysis, first introduced by Japanese rice farmers in the eighteenth century. Trader Steve Nison was the first to introduce candlestick charting to the West when his bestselling book on this method was published.

Once Nison's book was released, traders flocked to candlestick charts and never looked back. Many traders discovered that candlesticks were visually appealing and provided more actionable trade setups than a two-dimensional bar chart.

"The Japanese say that every candlestick line tells a story," Nison told me. "By using candlesticks, you can visually see who is in control of the market at the time the candlestick is formed."

The great thing about candlesticks is that they are not lagging (they don't give late signals) like traditional indicators. Candlesticks are all about evaluating the "here and now."

Traders like candlesticks because their signals are instantaneous. Many traders use this tool to spot potential reversals or to warn of unsafe conditions. If their analysis is correct, traders can get in or out of their positions before the market turns.

One fascinating feature of candlesticks is that they reflect behavior psychology. By studying candlestick patterns, you can measure the mood of the overall market or individual stocks. That means detecting human emotions including fear, greed, desperation, and indecision. It may be hard to believe, but all these emotions and more can be seen in a candlestick pattern.

The best way to use candlesticks is in conjunction with other technical indicators. For example, when volatility is low, sometimes traditional indicators are not as effective. During those times it makes sense to use candlesticks.

On the other hand, one of the criticisms of candlesticks is that they don't give specific entry or exit price targets. This is another reason why combining Western technical analysis with Eastern candlesticks is a very powerful way to analyze stocks.

Just as it's necessary to first learn the basics of any other tool, it's important to gain at least a basic candlestick education before using this method. In this chapter, I begin with candlestick basics and then move to candlestick patterns. Along the way, I provide a number of trading strategies and tactics using candlesticks.

CANDLESTICK BASICS

Candlesticks use two-dimensional bodies to show the range between the opening and closing stock price during any given time period. The low and high prices are plotted as a single line (the *shadow*). The price range between the opening and closing prices is plotted as a narrow rectangle (the *real body*).

Instead of comparing prices using technical indicators, traders who use candlesticks can visually see the price range using colors and shapes. Due to their popularity, candlesticks are available in almost every charting software package, and are often the default on many charts.

There are four components of a candlestick: *high*, *low*, *open*, and *close*. With these four outcomes, many different combinations are displayed on a chart.

Figure 8.1 shows the four components of a candlestick.

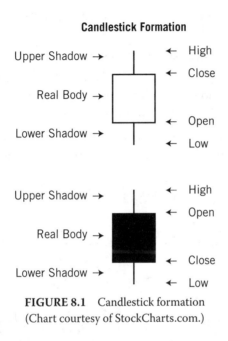

FIGURE 8.1 Candlestick formation
(Chart courtesy of StockCharts.com.)

The key to learning candlesticks is observing how parts of the candlestick interact with each other. Most importantly, watch how they change shape, color, and size. Those are the clues that help you to discover the mood of the market or determine when a reversal is imminent. Candlesticks help warn of potential threats or give the all-clear signal.

Candlestick Colors

The candlestick chart displays different colors such as green (bullish) and red (bearish), but how the colors are displayed depends on your brokerage software, which can be customized. In this book, you will see solid or hollow candlesticks (see Figure 8.2).

When do the basic candlestick colors occur?

- Green candlesticks occur when the close is *higher* than the previous close.
- Red candlesticks occur when the close is *below* the previous close.
- Solid candlesticks occur when the current close is *lower* than the same time period's opening price.
- Hollow candlesticks occur when the current closing price is *higher* than the same time period's opening price.

Figure 8.2 is an example of a candlestick chart.

FIGURE 8.2   Candlestick chart
(Chart courtesy of StockCharts.com.)

CANDLESTICK ANALYSIS

Studying the shape of the candlestick, the length of its lines, and whether the real body is hollow or solid reveals whether the bulls or bears are winning the battle.

In addition, a candlestick has different shapes that stretch and move as the stock moves higher and lower. The patterns created from the candlestick provide clues to future market direction. It also helps traders determine the strength or weakness of the buying or selling.

Trading volume helps confirm the validity of the price movement. There is a ton of information contained in one candlestick chart, proving the old adage that a picture is worth a thousand words.

> **HINT:** Ultimately, you want to use candlesticks to find answers to the following four questions: (1) Where does the stock price open? (2) Where does it close? (3) Where does it open and close compared with what it did the prior day? (4) What were the high and low prices of the day?

The Real Body

The thick or rectangular portion of the candlestick is called the *real body*. It displays the range between the opening and closing stock price. For "candlestickers" (a name I made up), it's important to understand the relationship between the open and close.

Another way to think about the candlestick body is as a place where bulls and bears fight for control, similar to a mosh pit, as one of my trading friends described it.

Sometimes the real body is long, and sometimes it is short. A *long body* indicates that one side clearly dominated. For example, long green candlesticks reflect strong buying pressure, while long red candlesticks reflect strong selling pressure.

If you notice short candlesticks, the chances are good that prices are consolidating, that is, not moving very far in either direction.

A *short body* suggests that the bulls and bears fought but neither side dominated. "We get nervous when the real body gets smaller and smaller because it means that supply and demand are becoming more equal," Nison explains.

> **HINT:** Sometimes there is no body at all, meaning the difference between the open and close is so insignificant (perhaps only a few pennies) that the body appears as a "hash" mark.

Watch the Open and Close

It should be clear that the most important parts of the day are the open and close. During the first five minutes of the trading day, the candlestick may not load immediately. As mentioned earlier, those first five minutes are fondly known as "amateur hour" because so many unseasoned and emotional traders are frantically buying or selling. It's easy to get fooled.

Only the Shadow Knows

The line that juts out from the real body is called the *shadow* (also known as the *wick*). Studying the length of the shadow quickly tells you who may be in charge, the bulls or the bears.

Shadows reflect the highs or lows of the day. For example, a *long upper shadow* indicates that the day's high was well above the open and close (bullish). Conversely, a *long lower shadow* indicates that the day's low was well below the open and close (bearish). The shadow gives you a lot of important clues.

Figure 8.3 shows the long upper shadow and long lower shadow.

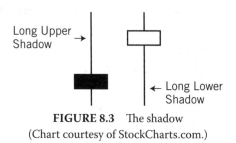

FIGURE 8.3 The shadow
(Chart courtesy of StockCharts.com.)

CANDLESTICK PATTERNS

There are over a hundred candlestick patterns, but you don't need all, or even most, of them. Learning a few of the most common patterns is all that you need to successfully use candlestick charts.

One of the easiest ways to find many of the candlestick patterns is to run a scan on your brokerage software. After the computer finds the patterns, it will help you learn which ones to use for your trading.

> **NOTE:** If you do not know how to do this, ask your brokerage if it has scanning software that detects candlestick patterns.

I'm going to discuss a few of the most interesting candlestick patterns (not necessarily the most popular). If you can recognize only a handful at first, that would be fantastic. (For readers who want to learn even more about candlesticks, look in the "Resources" section for information about Steve Nison's groundbreaking book.)

The Doji: An Indecisive Pattern

One of the most popular and recognizable patterns is the *doji*. It appears so often on a chart that some beginners overtrade when they see the pattern. Warning: Seeing a doji doesn't mean it's an actionable trade.

The doji is characterized by small thin lines and an equal opening and closing price. Put another way, it has no *real body*, only a cross. That cross means there is indecision between the bears and bulls. If you see one, be cautious about buying stocks at that moment.

There are two kinds of doji: bullish doji and bearish doji. As you can guess, a green doji candle is bullish. A red doji is bearish.

The doji pattern appears because buyers and sellers are fighting it out for pennies, one of the reasons that the doji range is so tight and volatility is so compressed. More than likely, it means that momentum is slowing but not reversing. The market appears unsure about which direction to go.

Think of the doji pattern as a signal to pause. A wise approach is to wait for the next candle to form before making buy or sell decisions. Some beginners make the mistake of jumping on the doji too early when they should have waited.

HINT: Western technical analysts might refer to the doji pattern as "consolidation." Nevertheless, be careful when a doji appears, as a reversal is possible.

Figure 8.4 shows what a doji looks like on a stock chart.

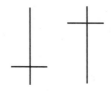

FIGURE 8.4   The doji
(Chart courtesy of StockCharts.com.)

Note that the dojis in Figure 8.4 have a small real body and small upper and lower shadows. The opening and closing prices are equal, and the cross forms the doji.

The doji is so fascinating because it may be setting up for a massive bullish or bearish reversal while it is pausing. That's how some traders get caught on the wrong side! After recognizing the doji, they think they know in which direction the market will go next. When wrong, they are trapped in a losing trade.

ADVANCED HINT: In addition to the "traditional" doji, there are four other types: *long-legged*, *dragonfly*, *gravestone*, and *4-price*. These are useful only for candlestick experts; for now, work with only the traditional doji.

Before introducing a few more candlestick patterns, to help you minimize risk, let's discuss some of the disadvantages of candlesticks.

False Signals and Other Candlestick Problems

One of the advantages of candlesticks is that they give early signals. However, like any other chart pattern, candlesticks are not 100 percent accurate. False or conflicting signals occur routinely. When that happens, the wisest move is to trade fewer shares or move to the sidelines until the signs are clearer.

It's also common for traders to pounce on a trade too quickly based on only one candlestick pattern. For example, they may think they see a doji and immediately think a reversal is coming. Then they sell short a stock and are disappointed when the trade doesn't work.

Only you can determine the validity of any signal after confirming with other indicators, and most importantly, by patiently waiting for other candlestick patterns to emerge. Wait until the entire candlestick story unfolds rather than stepping into a trade too early.

Finally, as mentioned earlier, don't make the mistake of relying *only* on candlesticks or *only* on technical patterns. Instead, use both.

Bearish Marubozu: Danger Ahead

This relatively rare but abnormal candlestick pattern is all body and no upper or lower shadow. If you see the marubozu pattern on a chart, don't panic, but take notice.

The *bearish marubozu* is a warning candle that should not be ignored. As one of my trader friends said, "It sticks out like a sore thumb. Don't mess with it because all hell may break loose."

This bearish pattern develops because the opening was the highest price of the day and the closing was the lowest price of the day. This results in strong selling pressure all day with very few buyers.

Begin by looking at volume at the bottom of the chart. Strong volume suggests that the selling pressure is the real deal. Because this bearish candlestick rarely reverses, it might be prudent to get out of your long positions now, because the crowd is selling.

Some traders may be tempted to initiate a short position as soon as the marubozu appears, but that is a risky move. Confirm with technical indicators, including support and resistance, that the stock is breaking down before you decide to short or sell long positions.

Figure 8.5 shows what a marubozu candlestick pattern looks like on a chart.

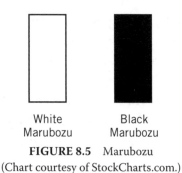

White
Marubozu

Black
Marubozu

FIGURE 8.5　Marubozu
(Chart courtesy of StockCharts.com.)

Spinning Top: Time to Take a Break

The *spinning top* looks similar to a doji, and like the doji, it warns of a potential reversal. This is especially true after a previously strong move. Unlike the cross configuration of the doji, however, the spinning top has a small, square-shaped body.

Think of the spinning top like a child's toy. It's another pause pattern that is neither bullish nor bearish. There is little volatility nor much trading activity. As with the doji, it's wise to wait on the sidelines until the next candlestick pattern appears, which should provide more precise clues.

Bearish Harami

While a *harami* can be bullish or bearish, the two-candle *bearish harami* is more significant, giving signals that alarm some traders. This pattern (a long white candle followed by a small black candle), suggests that there is a risk of a downside reversal.

> **HINT:** The smaller the candle, the higher the odds of a reversal. If you see this candlestick pattern, watch it closely, but don't act immediately. Be patient and wait for another candlestick for confirmation.

Bullish Engulfing Pattern

The bullish *engulfing pattern* (Figure 8.6) is the opposite of the bearish harami. This reliable two-candle pattern is likely to signal an upside reversal. It tends to occur during a downtrend, but on the second day, it reverses direction.

On the chart, you can see that the bulls have taken control (based on the fact that the hollow candlestick closes higher than the previous day's close and "engulfs" or overlaps the solid candlestick). This is a bullish signal. Increased volume confirms that the bullish trend is intact.

FIGURE 8.6 Bullish engulfing
(Chart courtesy of StockCharts.com.)

The Hammer

Another popular candlestick pattern is the *hammer*. The regular hammer is bullish. If the stock trades much lower than its opening price but rallies to close near or above its opening price, it may be a hammer. To qualify for that chart pattern, the shadow must be at least twice as long as the body.

Put another way, the stock has been falling so much that a bottom has formed, attracting buyers and creating a price reversal.

Morning Star

This candlestick pattern is used to identify a potential trend reversal. After a downtrend, you should see at least three green candlesticks. This signifies a bullish reversal. If you can confirm the bullish trend with technical indicators, it may be an actionable trade. Verify that volume is increasing, because that will confirm the strength of the move.

Dark Cloud Cover

Dark cloud cover is a bearish reversal pattern that helps identify market tops. It is significant because it shows a shift in momentum from positive to negative. It shows that buyers are giving up while sellers are gaining confidence. Typically, traders wait until the next day before making trades based on this pattern.

Dark cloud cover consists of two candles. The first candle continues the uptrend. It is long and bullish. The second candle opens above the first candle's high price but closes below the opening price. This is a bearish pattern.

IDENTIFYING CANDLESTICK PATTERNS

If you are new to candlesticks, your head may be spinning from all these patterns. Obviously, this is not something you can feel comfortable with in just a few days. The best advice I can give is to take your time and study only one pattern at a time.

For example, start with the doji and try to identify it on a chart using various stocks. Next, increase the number of patterns that you try to identify. I should emphasize that you are in the "chart recognition" stage, not the trading stage.

As you recognize patterns, learn what each candle represents and think about how you would make a trade. When you believe that you can recognize a pattern and understand its purpose, it may be time to make practice trades in your broker's simulated trading program.

CHART PATTERNS: FROM DOUBLE BOTTOMS TO TRIANGLES

If you just finished reading about candlestick patterns, I recommend taking a break before reading this sidebar, which introduces a number of popular chart patterns.

The theory behind patterns is that because market participants repeat the same trading behaviors, patterns occur repeatedly. Although not foolproof, acting on patterns works often enough to attract professional traders. The goal is to gain an edge over other traders, and identifying chart patterns is one way to do so.

Three of the most common patterns in classic (or Western) technical analysis are the *double top*, *double bottom*, and *head and shoulders*. I covered these patterns in my previous book, *Understanding Stocks*, but I will do a quick review below.

I'll also revisit a few of the more advanced patterns including the *triangle*, *flag*, *pennant*, and *wedge*. These patterns often appear on charts and give bullish or bearish setups. Experienced traders use them to attain clues to what may happen in the future.

One reason that traders utilize chart patterns is that so many of them turn into actionable trades. For example, it has been reported that more than 70 percent of the time, when a *descending triangle* is identified, the next move will be higher.

Trading from patterns is based on probabilities, which means there are going to be false signals. "Seeing" these patterns develop on a chart is not a skill that everyone has. Some traders are more visual, while others are more mathematical. There is no right answer for which approach is better for you.

Double Bottom (Bullish Pattern: Looks Like a W)

The double bottom is an easily recognizable stock pattern that shows up repeatedly on a chart. The pattern is especially easy to spot when looking at the overall market such as the Dow or S&P 500.

The double bottom pattern looks like a W. The stock or index falls to a support level, moves higher, and returns to, but not through, support. Failure to move through support is when the stock turns from a potentially bearish pattern into a bullish pattern.

Keep in mind that the double bottom pattern can develop quickly or may require several weeks or months. Technicians look at increased volume when the stock price rises from the second bottom as confirmation that the pattern is valid.

Consistent with all other chart patterns, the W on a chart doesn't necessarily mean it is an actionable signal. In fact, it could be a serious mistake to take a position solely because you recognize a double bottom pattern on a stock chart.

Double Top (Bearish Pattern: Looks Like an M)

The double top is another common bearish pattern that is the opposite of the double bottom. It has two peaks around the same price level (resistance). After an uptrend, when the stock price has failed to break resistance after two attempts, the uptrend is likely to have ended.

When the stock cannot break through the second leg's high price and declines, the double top pattern is complete. Look for increased volume as the stock price falls, thereby confirming the bearish pattern.

Head and Shoulders Reversal Pattern

One of the most reliable patterns is the *head and shoulders* reversal pattern. It indicates that buying has stopped at the top of the uptrend and is poised to reverse direction. If you look at the chart in Figure 8.7, you'll see that the pattern really does look like a head and shoulders.

FIGURE 8.7   Head and shoulders
(Chart courtesy of StockCharts.com.)

In Figure 8.7, the stock moves higher but pulls back to form the left shoulder. It then moves higher to form the head, which appears bullish because the price moved above the previous (left shoulder) high. It then falls back to support, or the neckline (the alignment of the two support levels).

The stock rises again to form the right shoulder but fails to break resistance (the high price of the head). Keep your eye on the neckline because when the stock breaks below that level, the chances are good that there is money to be made by taking a short position or exiting a long position.

The broken neckline confirms that the upward trend has ended and reversed. It is common for volume to decrease as the pattern develops. Once the stock falls below the neckline, volume may increase if the stock price plunges (this is what technicians expect to see).

Now that you are familiar with some of the most basic patterns, let's study a few more patterns that appear often on a chart. These are not as popular with beginners, but they are worth learning.

Triangle

A triangle is part of a continuation pattern. It simply means that a stock is continuing to move in the same direction, perhaps pausing (consolidating) along the way, but the trend remains intact as volatility continues to compress. The triangle can be bullish, bearish, or neutral. Most importantly, traders use these patterns to help forecast what may happen in the future.

There are three types of triangles: *ascending*, *descending*, and *symmetrical*.

- **Ascending triangle (bullish).** The bullish ascending triangle pattern occurs when two trendlines converge to form a triangle. The point where the two converging lines meet completes the pattern. As a result, the stock price moves higher and pushes above resistance.

    This is an eye-catching pattern for many traders because the odds of a breakout increase when the stock price moves higher.

    NOTE: Volume should increase as the bullish triangle pattern is formed. Figure 8.8 is an example of the bullish ascending triangle.

FIGURE 8.8 Ascending triangle
(Chart courtesy of StockCharts.com.)

- **Descending triangle (bearish).** The bearish descending triangle is an inverted image of the ascending triangle. The stock price is falling below support and making new lows. The point where the two converging lines meet forms the triangle. As a result, the stock price moves lower and pushes below support. Short sellers are poised to pounce when they detect a descending triangle, as the odds of a breakdown increase.

- **Symmetrical triangle (neutral).** In technical analysis, *flags* and *pennants* are part of the triangle family. Many technicians believe that pennants and flags give the most reliable signals. Because they are continuation patterns, stocks tend to move sideways first before continuing to trend higher or lower.

  NOTE: Triangles are considered an intermediate pattern, which means a triangle can take a month or longer to form. The flag and pennant, on the other hand, are considered short-term patterns that may take one to three weeks to form.

Flag

This is a short-term continuation pattern that shows a brief pause after a previously sharp move in the stock price. Traders maintain that this pattern means the market is "catching its breath" before taking off again later. The flag is considered to be a consistent pattern that rarely reverses direction.

Increasing volume confirms that the pattern is formed, and that the trend is valid. Although the flag looks similar to a pennant, a flag's trendlines are parallel. Actually, when you see the pattern on a chart (Figure 8.9), it really does look like a flag (and even has its own flagpole!).

NOTE: A bearish flag appears as an inverted flag on a stock chart.

FIGURE 8.9 Flag
(Chart courtesy of StockCharts.com.)

Pennant

The short-term pennant looks similar to the flag except that its trendlines converge to create a pennant rather than a flag. In other words, the pennant itself is more horizontal than the flag, but its top and bottom edges slope toward each other.

Both short-term patterns (the flag and pennant) represent a pause in the current trend. Verify that volume increases as the pattern is formed, confirming that the trend is valid.

NOTE: At first, volume should be very light with both patterns. After the breakout, volume increases.

Wedge

The wedge is similar to the triangle because two converging trendlines join to form an *apex* (or point). Both typically take one to three months to form (although the wedge may take longer).

The main difference between a triangle and wedge is the slant (angle) of the trendlines. The trendline of a rising wedge slants downward (bearish reversal pattern), while the trendline of a falling wedge slants upward (bullish reversal pattern). This is not a typo: The wedge and triangle have converging trendlines that slant in the opposite direction of the current trend (just as with a flag pattern).

NOTE: If you are fascinated by these chart patterns and want to learn even more about them, you may want to read the book *Technical Analysis of the Financial Markets* by John Murphy. All patterns discussed in this chapter plus many more (including candlesticks) are included in his book.

In addition, the website StockCharts.com has a detailed description of the candlestick patterns as well as every chart pattern and indicator included in this book. Go to ChartSchool (school.stockcharts.com) for a first-rate chart education.

The financial website Investopedia also has an excellent description of each of the patterns included in this chapter.

· · · · · · · ·

Now that you have a thorough understanding and insights into indicators, oscillators, and candlesticks, it's time to apply what you've learned. In Part Three you will learn a number of trading strategies including trend and momentum trading strategies. I think you'll enjoy reading about these methods.

TREND AND MOMENTUM STRATEGIES

N ow that you know how to use indicators, oscil- lators, and candlesticks, you should be ready for trend and momentum strategies. No matter which time frame is used, the chances are good that you will use one of these trading approaches. In Part Three, you will learn both.

I will begin by discussing one of the most popular investment and trade strategies in the world (and for good reason): *trend trading,* or *trend following.* Many proponents of trend trading made fortunes using some of the ideas presented in this chapter. The strategy is deceptively easy to understand, but it's not always easy to make a profit.

CHAPTER 9

SHORT-TERM TREND TRADING

Many books have been written about the advantages of being a trend trader. The idea is to depend on the strength of the trend to continue moving the index or stock price higher (or lower). Then you hop on board (and tag along for the ride) by making a trade in the same direction as the trend. The goal is to stay with the trend until it ends and to avoid positions that buck that trend.

As you probably know, there are three primary trends: uptrend, downtrend, and sideways trend. Trend traders go long during uptrends and either get short or sit out downtrends.

Sideways trends are typically the most difficult to manage. The vast majority of trend traders take a wait-and-see attitude during sideways trends until the stock price breaks out in one direction or the other.

Trend trading can be used as both a short-term and long-term strategy. In this chapter, we are focused on short-term trend trading. However, the length of the trade is not determined in advance. Trend traders stay with their positions until the trend ends.

When you catch a trend in its early stages, it's exciting. There is the potential for huge gains when you have the discipline to stick with the trend. You can follow the trend from minutes to years. That is why following the trend is so popular, as long as you have the discipline to stay the course.

Trend traders are pleased to own stocks that lumber along in an upward direction even when momentum and volatility are subdued. Successful trend traders must be patient while waiting for the trend to develop.

Sometimes the trend continues in one direction for a long time period. At other times, it fizzles out. The ideal stock for a trend trader is one that continues in a single direction, and with any luck, for days, weeks, or months. During these times, trend followers reap large rewards.

I have done extensive research on trend trading strategies, and I use these strategies myself. I have discovered that not everyone in the trading community agrees on the precise definition of a "trend." For our purposes, investors follow long-term trends. True trend trading is an all-in or all-out strategy.

On the other hand, short-term traders typically follow short-term trends (and "never the twain shall meet"). Obviously, these short-term traders rely on technical analysis to enter or exit positions. They may also hedge or scale into or out of a trade.

Keep in mind that in theory hedging and scaling violate the trend trading rulebook. However, there is nothing wrong with modifying this strategy or any other introduced in this book. As long as it brings profits, then keep doing what works for you.

I am giving you the facts as I have interpreted them, but for those who want to learn more about trend trading, I recommend doing even more of your own research. Consider this as a friendly introduction to this popular strategy.

LIKE A MAGNET

Try to visualize a large magnet that draws in billions of investment dollars. As the stock price moves higher, more money is drawn to that magnet. If you were able to join that trend, it would be a great way to make money over the long term.

Therefore, if you identify a trend as it is developing and ride it higher or lower, then exit that trend with a profit, you might like this strategy. The problem, as you may know, is that in the short term, trends are not always obvious, nor are they stable. There are numerous false breakouts, reversals, pullbacks, and rallies. In other words, trend followers incur numerous whipsaws and small losses.

It is not surprising that investors ignore short-term fluctuations (volatility) as they buy and hold. Actually, it is an easier and less stressful way to invest in the stock market. Don't get me wrong: I'm not saying that buy and hold investing is better. My point is that it's less demanding.

On the other hand, you may be here because you want to trade stocks, and not necessarily to buy and hold them. As I wrote earlier, trend trading works with both long and short time periods. Fortunately, traders have a strong ally: indicators and oscillators.

Those technical tools help to identify trends, and determine when to get in and out and when a trending stock has gotten so overbought or oversold that you should prepare to exit soon. Consider these tools as your friends.

Investors who don't believe in technical analysis are limiting themselves. Essentially, they are hoping their stocks and the overall market keep trending higher indefinitely. Sometimes their hopes are fulfilled, but many times they are not.

In reality, there are times when the market or a stock is uncooperative and doesn't follow the script. That's when you'll be glad you have studied trend-following indicators such as moving averages and MACD. They are designed to keep you on the prevailing side of the trend.

> **NOTE:** Sometimes there is no trend at all (this is called *consolidation*). When that happens, sit tight, because the trend could pivot in either direction.

To help get you started as a trend trader, the sidebar below provides a list of the bullish technical signals to look for when using short-term trend trading strategies. The idea is to find a buy or sell signal generated by your favorite indicators (preferably at least two).

TECHNICAL TREND TRADING SIGNALS (BULLISH)

- **Moving averages.** You are looking for stocks to move above their 50-, 100-, and 200-day moving averages (or use shorter periods if you are a short-term trader).
- **MACD.** When the MACD line is above the zero line and the MACD line crosses above the 9-day signal line, this may be an actionable bullish signal.
- **Support and resistance.** The stock price must be above support and confirmed by other technical indicators. As a trend trader, ride the uptrend as long as you can. As long as the stock price is above its moving averages (support levels), there is no urgent need to sell.

· · · · · · · · ·

TECHNICAL SIGNALS THAT A TREND HAS BROKEN

Trend traders tend to hold stocks as long as the trend is moving in the right direction. However, if a trend breaks, that is when most short-term trend traders look for an exit.

There are a number of clues that confirm that the short-term trend has broken. It is a red flag when the stock price violates a major support level such as the 20-, 50-, or 100-day moving average and fails to rise back above it. As you may recall, the previous support level now acts as resistance.

Another clue that a trend may have ended (or broken) is when momentum hits a proverbial wall. Remember from our earlier discussion that momentum turns before the stock price. Therefore, if momentum stops expanding, that is a clue that a trend change is possible. Like a stock detective, you must put all the clues together to identify potential trend reversals.

Keep in mind that these are only clues. They alert you that a reversal is possible, but by no means are they guaranteed signals. While technical analysis is a science, reading and interpreting the signals is more of an art. Everyone may be looking at the same signals, but only those who can decipher them correctly will make it to the winner's circle.

WHEN TREND TRADING FAILS TO WORK

Trend trading, as with any other strategy, isn't perfect. For example, many trends fail to develop and fizzle out early. Moreover, timing when to enter a trend can be a frustrating experience, as stock prices can fluctuate wildly. Many times, there is no trend, so you're left with no trade. If that happens, wait patiently for other opportunities, and don't rush into another trade.

The bad news for some traders is that trendless stock markets sometimes last not just for days or weeks but for much longer. Patience is needed during these times, as well as for finding a strategy that works.

HINT: One strategy that does work during trendless markets is *selling covered calls*, which you can read about in Chapter 19.

Now that you have a better understanding and overview of trend trading, this is the perfect time for me to introduce a trend that is one of the strongest and most powerful in the financial markets, but few discuss it or even know its name.

THE STEAMROLLER: THE MOST POWERFUL STOCK PATTERN IN THE MARKET

There is a short-term trend that develops in the morning, then builds strength at midday and becomes unstoppable in the afternoon. This trend, when identified, can bring the most money with the least effort. Technicians call it a *trend day*.

Since trend day is such a boring description for this big money-maker, I renamed it the *Steamroller*, because it is a more accurate definition of this chart pattern.

It's true that if you tell stock market technicians about the Steamroller, they will give you a confused look. In fact, many trend trading purists, some who are extremely picky about definitions, will be annoyed if you use the name Steamroller. You should also know there is some disagreement within the trading community on what a "trend day" really is.

Let's focus on trading this amazing pattern. If all you did was trade the Steamroller, you could make decent profits. In fact, making profits is all that should matter to you.

The Steamroller

The Steamroller can be bullish (*Bullish Steamroller*) or bearish (*Bearish Steamroller*). One unique characteristic of the Steamroller is that it starts off slowly and then builds strength and momentum during the day, rejecting all attempts to slow or reverse it. The power of the Steamroller is so great that it is nearly unstoppable.

In Figure 9.1, the stock barreled higher all day, rising above its moving average on the daily chart and confirming that it was a true Steamroller.

NOTE: This stock, Tesla, was on a roll for the next five days, running over any short sellers who tried to stop its upward trajectory.

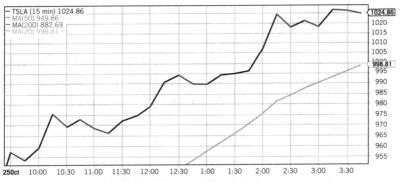

FIGURE 9.1 The Steamroller
(Chart Courtesy of StockCharts.com.)

The Bullish Steamroller

Typically, the Steamroller develops in the futures market (the pre-market), pointing to a strong bullish opening, probably up more than 1 or 2 percent. The odds are good that a Bullish Steamroller will emerge that day, and occasionally within the first hour. If you have never experienced this strong trend, it may blow your socks off, so to speak. After the market opens at 9:30 a.m. ET, the stock price rises forcefully. That is the first clue it's a potential Steamroller.

NOTE: It usually takes a while for a Steamroller to develop. Don't make the rookie mistake of piling into an uptrend in the first few minutes. Often, the market or a stock starts off strongly but then loses steam within minutes (what I call a one-minute wonder).

Wait at least an hour or more before proclaiming a Steamroller, as it could fluctuate. There may also be head fakes and brief pullbacks. If it's a true Bullish Steamroller, it will shrug off all attempts to reverse its direction and then power higher.

Midday

As mentioned earlier, it's possible that you can identify a Bullish Steamroller in the first hour, but not always. Be patient and watch as this trend builds up strength with an occasional hiccup. If it's a true Steamroller, momentum keeps building, so that by midday the trend is so powerful, nothing can stop it. If you had identified it early enough and were able to buy into it, then you will enjoy the fruits of your labor.

Once a Steamroller is established, do not bet against it. Those who do may regret their decision. This trend is relentless.

The Steamroller should pick up steam in the afternoon and will be resilient right into the close. Along the way, it attracts more followers such as day traders, investors, and algos. This heavy buying pressure lifts all the leading stocks higher, like a tide lifting all ships.

Steamroller Days

You may be asking that if the Bullish Steamroller is such an obvious moneymaker, why doesn't everyone buy on a *Steamroller day*. The answer is simple: They do! Many pros pounce on this trend once it's identified, and in fact, that is one of the reasons that the Bullish Steamroller starts off slowly and then picks up momentum at midday.

Some money managers detect which stocks or indexes are attracting money (order flow), and swoop in with buy orders. Then algos jump into the trade, powering the market even higher.

Knowledgeable retail traders may join in with buy orders and potentially profit from this powerful trend, too. If you catch the Steamroller at the right time with your technical tools, you can make profits in the short and long term. The odds are with the longs, so you are better off joining the party or risk getting run over. This is one of those times when it is essential to trade with the trend.

The only losers are those who attempt to short this relentless beast. Even professional short sellers who step in front of the rising tide may get steamrolled. In fact, trapped short sellers are forced to buy to cover their losing positions, forcing the market even higher.

In the afternoon, the only way this monstrous blob can reverse direction is if some unexpected, extraordinarily bad news comes out to reverse the trajectory.

NOTE: Sometimes the market starts off strongly at the open (up more than 1 or 2 percent) but doesn't move higher that day. This price action is *not* a Steamroller. A true Steamroller picks up steam throughout the entire day. Although Bullish Steamrollers don't occur that often, they are worth the wait. They are much more common during bull markets, while the Bearish Steamroller is more common during bear markets.

HINT: One unique characteristic of a Steamroller is that while it is trending higher in the morning, there tends to be little volatility. This is one of the reasons why so many traders misread the Steamroller signals and don't participate (or worse, short it). Even though volatility is subdued, the power underneath the trend is tremendous.

Why so much power? That is because many on Wall Street are piling in, including institutions that may be hedging off short positions or chasing performance. Once these large institutions go on a buying spree, it's unlikely they will sell soon, one of the reasons a Steamroller can continue for much longer than a few days.

End of the Month or Quarter

There are certain days that should be on your calendar. Those occur at the end of the month and the end of the quarter (the last three days). On these days, hedge funds, mutual funds, and institutions use a strategy affectionately known in the industry as "window dressing." These days are usually favorable to anyone trading the Steamroller.

This is when fund managers must show clients they own many winning stocks with few losers. Most importantly, the fund managers must prove that they beat their benchmark (such as the S&P 500). On these special window dressing days, some winning stocks are pushed to unreasonably high levels.

It's incredible to see this phenomenon play out when certain stocks are thrust to overbought levels right before the quarter ends. Because of window dressing, the odds are good that some stocks will rise on these days. In the financial industry, fund managers prefer to say they are searching for *alpha*, or the excess return above a specific benchmark by which the fund's performance is measured (such as the S&P 500 index).

Any traders with a short position who are unaware of this event may find themselves losing extra money when shorts are "squeezed" (when shorts are forced to cover their losing positions because the stock is rising so rapidly). Those forced purchases drive prices even higher.

When institutions have piled into winners, the risk of a reversal is slim. At the same time, because of window dressing, losing stocks are severely punished.

When to Sell a Steamroller

Even with a Steamroller, it's possible to mishandle the trade and lose money. It happens to veteran traders or to anyone who is overconfident. While it's prudent to buy into a Steamroller (it's recommended that you scale into it), it's challenging to exit at an appropriate time.

A short-term trader tends to sell within the same day or the next day. Weekly or swing traders often exit by Friday. If you earn profits on a Steamroller day, you might feel emboldened, but it's not yet the time to celebrate. It's possible that this lucrative trade is a one-day wonder and will reverse the next day.

During a bull market, there is a good chance that the Steamroller "has legs"; that is, it will continue moving for longer than a day but probably with decreasing intensity. Only you can decide whether to hold a few more days or sell within the same day. This decision depends on your strategic plan and goal for the trade.

Don't Short a Steamroller

I hope I made it clear that most traders love a Bullish Steamroller, except for short sellers. My advice: Don't short a Steamroller. That is how many short sellers end their careers and decimate their accounts.

One common mistake is misreading the indicators. At first, RSI rises, confirming the strength of the move. As the Steamroller gains traction, RSI (and other bounded oscillators such as Bollinger Bands) may go off the charts. These indicators may even yield readings that reach their threshold limits (called *burying the needle*).

This is when some short sellers believe the market or a stock "can't go any higher." They are wrong: A Bullish Steamroller rejects any attempt by short sellers to stall or reverse its direction. Short sellers will get mowed down if they try.

Steamroller Trading Hints

A Bullish Steamroller appears infrequently. It is not designed to be traded every day, but only on the days when everything (technical analysis as well as the overall market environment) lines up correctly.

If all you did was trade this one pattern, you might be able to make a good living as a trader. The key is identifying it correctly and entering at the right time. Have a plan prepared, and follow your plan the next time a Steamroller appears.

It may seem like a slam dunk to make a profit on a Steamroller day. In fact, it takes patience and good judgment to profit from a Steamroller even if it seems easy and obvious (in hindsight). It also takes skill to identify this pattern in time to profit from it. Many traders get head-faked into abandoning the trade too early.

The worst mistake that many traders make is proclaiming a Steamroller too soon before it has been confirmed. Wait patiently for a Steamroller to develop before buying.

Finally, don't confuse the Steamroller with a stock that gaps up strongly at the open. Stocks or indexes that gap at the open are *not* Steamrollers. As I wrote earlier, stocks that gap up at the open and reverse direction within minutes are one-minute wonders. I discuss trading gapping stocks in Chapter 12.

· · · · · · · · ·

Now that you have learned how to trade a variety of trends and stock patterns, it's time to rev up the engines and introduce you to a high-risk trade that appeals to traders: momentum trading.

As long as you are keenly aware of the risks of using this short-term strategy, then it may be something to consider. I warn you that while momentum trading can bring good-sized profits when you make a winning trade, it can damage your account if you overtrade or bet too much money on one position. However, if you like taking risks for the potential of a big reward, you'll like this strategy.

CHAPTER 10

MOMENTUM TRADING

I n this chapter, I introduce a high-risk but often highly profitable short-term strategy called *momentum trading*. It is a popular strategy, especially during bull markets, one of the reasons it deserves its own chapter.

Momentum (or "momo") traders need wild price swings amidst other traders' panic and euphoria to make money. They follow a trend, but unlike traditional trend traders, these buyers thrive on short-term momentum and volatility.

Sometimes momentum traders follow the trend, and sometimes they go against it (called *contrarian trading*). Momentum traders ride the coattails of institutions and retail investors in either direction as long as there is volatility and a strong trend.

Momo traders don't have time to waste. They want to make profits at warp speed and move to the next trade. They hold as long as they think they can until they decide that it's time to get out.

Day traders who use momo strategies always get out within the same day, no matter what. A few momentum traders may hold overnight but only until the momo runs out.

One thing is certain: This strategy is for highly skilled, experienced traders who are knowledgeable about technical analysis. Even more importantly, you must be able to manage risk. Specifically, you must have the ability to exit losing trades quickly. To use this strategy, you must have the discipline to trade responsibly and to obey your rules.

One of my trader friends compared this method to being a surfer riding a big, beautiful wave—until you fall off the board. You'd better know how to get back on the board, or you will drown.

It doesn't matter to momentum traders whether a stock or ETF is ridiculously overbought or oversold. What matters is the ability to keep riding the wave higher until it stalls, and then exit in time. It's not as easy as it sounds.

Momentum traders, especially beginners, make a lot of mistakes. It's understandable, because trying to make money in a highly charged, fast-moving, and complicated environment is difficult.

My purpose is not to curb your enthusiasm for momentum trading but to give you the facts based on my personal experience and research. You need to know you are entering a treacherous trading environment where it may seem deceptively easy to make a profit.

If you are determined to use these strategies, I will not try to change your mind. All I can suggest is that you enter this Wild West arena with the proper tools, mindset, and knowledge so that you have a fighting chance to succeed. In this chapter, I offer guidance.

> **NOTE:** An even more extreme momentum trade is *trading gaps*. I will discuss this high-risk, high-reward strategy in Chapter 12. Momentum trading is difficult enough—trading gaps is on another planet.

TREND TRADING VERSUS MOMENTUM TRADING

You may wonder what the difference is between a short-term trend trader and a momentum trader. Here is the primary difference: Momentum traders generally only buy when there is extreme volatility and strong momentum. They piggyback off momo and ride the stock higher (or lower).

Momentum trading is risky because high-flying stocks can stall and quickly reverse direction. Momentum traders often "chase performance" long after the price trend has been established.

Trend traders, as you learned in the previous chapter, don't need a fluctuating market to make money. In fact, long-term trend traders prefer a lower-volatility market environment. The main point is this: While both momentum traders and trend traders follow trends, their strategies are completely different.

RIDING THE WAVE

Just like trend followers, bullish momo traders ride the wave of institutional traders, algos, and retail traders who are buying stocks that are moving higher. The difference is that momo traders seek out fast-moving stocks and stay with them as long as they keep moving higher (or lower). They love using volatility to make money on the upside or downside.

As long as they choose the correct direction and take profits, it's possible to make fantastic short-term profits with this strategy. It's a beautiful feeling when you are on the right side of a strong uptrend.

I can't stress enough that this is an *intraday* strategy. Strong momentum doesn't usually last very long, and that's the reason these traders must book profits quickly. Since momo profits often occur within the first hour of the trading day, many momo traders are done before midday. That's a personal choice, however.

To be a performance-chasing momentum trader, you will probably buy at or near the top of a trend and piggyback onto order flow as high as it goes. Perhaps the stock has already moved higher by 5 or 6 percent in the first hour. As a momo trader, you may step in and try to ride it even higher.

HOW TO FIND MOMENTUM STOCKS

The good news about using this strategy is that momentum stocks are easy to find. Here are a few ideas:

- Find stocks that are at or near their 52-week highs. These stocks can be found on MarketWatch, CNN Money, Yahoo Finance, Google Finance, and Market Chameleon, to name a few.
- Find stocks that are trending higher (or lower if shorting) in the premarket. The most active stocks that are about to shoot out of the starting gate can be found on the websites mentioned above (among others).
- Run a scan on your broker's trading software. Most brokers give you the ability to scan for criteria such as premarket winners and losers, or whichever criteria you enter.
- Be attentive to stocks that are in the news before the market opens. Be careful, because some of these hot stocks may turn from a momentum trade to a gap trade, an even higher-risk, higher-reward strategy.

WHY MOMENTUM TRADING WORKS

Many momo traders depend on the power of the algos and institutions to push stocks to extreme levels in either direction. What retail traders don't always realize is that algos are not their friend. All they do is provide the liquidity that momo traders thrive on. It's the liquidity that makes this strategy work. Once that liquidity breaks, however, exit fast.

In other words, today the liquidity suppliers may be trading on your side. Tomorrow, they may be trading against you. They don't care about you or your account, so be cautious when using them to make money.

Many traders believe that volatility will make them big money. In reality, volatility is a double-edged sword because it cannot be controlled. When volatility is on your side and pushing your stocks higher, life is good, but when it turns against you, you'd better find the door fast.

The sidebar below includes specific signals to look for when trading momentum stocks.

MOMENTUM TECHNICAL SIGNALS

- **Moving averages.** You are looking for stocks to break above their 14-, 20-, 50-, and 100-day moving averages (but many momentum traders use even shorter time periods).
- **MACD.** You want momentum to be on your side (MACD must be above the zero line and above the 9-day signal line). In addition, look for bullish divergences, as they give the most meaningful signal (although the signal is slower than that provided by stochastics).
- **MACD histogram.** Look for the bars to get darker, a signal that momentum is increasing. As a momentum trader, you want to see momentum strengthen. Don't forget that momentum moves before prices, so be ready to abandon your position if momentum weakens.
- **Slow (or Fast) Stochastics.** You want %K and %D to move higher, but if they rise above 75 or 80 and cross (overbought), it's a sell signal. Momentum traders have to be extremely careful when stocks get overbought, as reversals are very common.
- **RSI.** Use RSI to identify overbought conditions and to confirm the strength of the uptrend. If RSI suddenly turns lower, it's possible the stock price is building downside momentum. It's

not necessarily a sell signal, but be careful. As a momentum trader, you can't hold an overbought stock position too long or you'll be trapped in a long position if it reverses.

- **Volatility.** If volatility is expanding (via Bollinger Bands or RSI), that is a positive sign for momentum traders. This often occurs when overbought stocks spike higher. It could explode to extreme levels, which is what momentum traders live for. Nevertheless, don't stay at the momo party for too long or you may get trapped. The first sign of trouble is when momentum begins to contract (Bollinger Bands narrow and volatility decreases). That is a red flag.
- **Support and resistance.** You are on the right side if you are long and the stock breaks above resistance levels. As a momo trader, ride the uptrend as long as you can, but be cautious.
- **Candlesticks.** The candlesticks are going to light up green while the stock is moving higher. However, be on the lookout for a series of red candlesticks, a sign that the stock price is reversing direction.

· · · · · · · ·

MOMO TRADING TIPS

For those who want to use momentum trading strategies, here are a few tips that you may find helpful:

- If you make so much money that you feel euphoric, that may be the time to get out of the trade before your gains are lost. Taking incremental gains before the stock reverses is a solid selling strategy.
- There is little room for error when using momentum strategies. You must pay close attention to your stocks at all times. Unfortunately, traditional hard stops may not work as well because many of these stocks move at lightning speed. You

often have to make spur-of-the-moment selling decisions, and you'd better be right. Having a plan and following it will cut down on mistakes.

• I recommend not juggling more than one or two positions at a time. It's hard enough to follow one of these stocks; following more than two could cause problems.

• Fundamentals such as P/E ratios, earnings, or intrinsic value are not useful to a momo trader. If anything, it distracts from making a trade. Momo traders only care about the speed of the move and how long they can remain on that wave.

WHAT, ME SELL?

Momentum traders have to get out of their positions quickly. Why? Because momentum is like a burst of energy that flames out after an uncertain time period (an exit point that is not easy to pinpoint). If momo traders don't realize that momentum is slowing and sell the position for a profit, it's likely they will be left holding the proverbial bag.

With momo trading, it is difficult to determine when to get out. Momo traders are always afraid the rug is going to be pulled out from under them, and they're right. The penalty for being long and wrong is severe. It's easy to lose money quickly.

There are millions of stories of traders who didn't get out in time after making incredible paper profits. When holding a momo position, the reversal often happens so fast that you almost never have enough time to escape. Watching a winning position turn into a loser is one of the worst experiences for your ego and trading account.

When entering into a fast-moving trade along with other momo traders, it can be excruciatingly difficult to exit with a gain (or exit without incurring large losses). Unfortunately, most retail momo traders believe that they can get out in time. They say it so often, they begin to believe it.

When your stock is moving at a shockingly fast speed, and you're making money, why spoil the fun and sell? Because that's exactly what you should do. You *don't* have a lot of time to get out.

Even worse, many of these same momo traders have no exit plan except to just ride the trend as long as possible and get out "in time." This is a big mistake! If you use this strategy, you must have an exit plan, target prices, and stop losses. If you don't, it is an accident waiting to happen.

Just so you don't forget, every momo trader should remember the following: *Time is not on your side.* Momentum positions have a funny way of reversing just before you were going to cash in your profits.

THE PSYCHOLOGY OF MOMENTUM TRADERS

Understanding the psychology of momentum traders helps you to understand the momentum strategy and perhaps keep you out of trouble. Momo traders have a strong desire to make fast money. They don't have the patience to invest and then wait around a year for their stocks to generate a 10 percent return. A year? Forget about it.

Momentum traders live for the moment, and so do their stocks. They don't just accept risk—they thrive on it. They are willing to take big chances for a big payoff. To them, the risk is worth the reward.

> **NOTE:** To make matters worse, some momentum traders are afflicted with "MOMO FOMO," the fear of missing out on the next momo trade.

Nervous Nellies

It's not surprising that many momo traders are constantly on edge. They're afraid to sell, but they're also afraid to hold too long. Ironically, it's the nervous momo traders who may survive.

On the other hand, if you're too complacent using this strategy and dismiss major losses with a shrug of the shoulder, your account may not survive for long. Having a laissez-faire attitude and not taking extraordinary steps to limit risk is a mistake you want to avoid.

NOTE: Professional momentum traders calculate potential losses in advance and only make the trade when the risk-reward profile is favorable.

Gamblers Beware

Unfortunately, traders with gambling personalities are often drawn to this strategy. For the sake of your account and your mental health, if that sounds like you, I urge that you use other strategies in this book. Gamblers' trading accounts have a short life expectancy.

If you insist on proceeding despite my suggestions, at first trade only a few shares while you learn this strategy. Perhaps you won't make a lot of money, but you won't lose much as you gain valuable experience.

It might sound like I am against momo trading. Not at all. It is a popular strategy that I have used myself. I am blunt about the risks to protect you from yourself. If you don't have excellent trading skills or the emotional fortitude to survive using this strategy, you are going to lose money. I don't want that to happen to you, so proceed at your own peril.

This is why momo traders must be disciplined, unemotional, and quick with their fingers. Your stops must be tighter, your exits faster, and your judgment sound. If you make a mistake and get trapped, the pain can be relentless. To avoid this fate, be on guard and do not get complacent during a momo trade.

On the flip side, some beginners who taste early success with momo strategies may feel euphoric after a series of winning trades. Instead of reducing the amount bet on the next trade, they make the common gambling mistake of betting it all. I don't have to tell you what happens: The next trade blows up, and their account is toast.

Again, you must know the cold hard truth if you plan to trade stocks, crypto, futures contracts, options, and currencies using momentum strategies.

This includes being honest with yourself. If you are losing a lot of money, or sleep, wake up to reality. Either find another strategy or take a long break until you figure out what went wrong.

Go for Small Wins

Perhaps the worst mistake that momo traders make is deluding themselves into believing that every trade will bring in fast profits. In their minds, they calculate all the gains they will receive without including potential losses (it's important to note that it's not just momo traders who make this mistake).

They are shocked when, instead of a series of small wins (singles), they have a series of small losses (death by a thousand cuts). Losing was not part of the calculation.

WHEN THE MOMO RUNS OUT

Another risk is that after having 10 or 11 or more consecutive profitable days, many momo traders believe they have discovered the secret to the universe. On the twelfth day, they let down their guard and liquidity disappears, and the trap door opens.

Before they have time to react, they are trapped in a bad position, losing a month of profits in a single trade. It's happened to many momo traders that I know.

I'd like to close this chapter on a positive note: If you are determined to succeed as a momentum trader, you can do it by following all the clues and trading signals in this chapter. Don't trade on margin, and most importantly: Practice, practice, practice.

. . . .

If you liked momentum trading, then you'll enjoy Part Four, where I introduce higher-risk, higher-reward trades. For your education and entertainment, I introduce day trading, trading gaps, cryptocurrency strategies, and the riskiest of all, trading penny stocks. Only disciplined traders need apply.

HIGH-RISK, HIGH-REWARD TRADING STRATEGIES

I f you are the kind of trader who thrives on taking risks for an opportunity to make big gains, Part Four is for you. You will be introduced to the high-octane strategies such as day trading (also called *intraday trading*), trading gaps, cryptocurrencies, and penny stocks.

Although these strategies are not for everyone, it is useful to understand these strategies even if you don't plan on using them right away. On occasion, there are times when day trading makes sense for anyone who has the discipline to follow the rules and indicators. On those days, you'll be glad you learned these tactics.

You will also learn about *trading gaps*, a special strategy aimed at traders who are willing to take extreme risks. I also help you understand cryptocurrencies and whether they are right for you.

As always, I stress the importance of controlling risk when using these strategies. Fasten your seatbelts as I introduce you to some of the wildest strategies in the financial markets. If you thrive on taking chances, you are in the right place.

CHAPTER 11

DAY TRADING STRATEGIES

*D*ay trading, or *intraday trading*, consists of entering a trade involving one or more stocks (or ETFs such as SPY, QQQ, and IWM) and exiting the trade on the same day. The holding period can be seconds, minutes, or hours. The goal is to make a trade, exit with a profit, and get a good night's sleep.

The lure of day trading is that you can make money before midday while at home in your sweatpants. As you'll see below, being a successful intraday trader takes incredible discipline and focus. While the idea of making money within minutes is enticing, it's also easy to lose money. I'll do my best to describe both the risks and the rewards.

Here's something that will surprise you: Of all the strategies introduced in Part Four, day trading is the least risky. I applaud you for wanting to learn about this fascinating strategy, but enter with your eyes wide open. A lot of things can go wrong.

While it's wonderful to dream of all the money you could make by day trading, it's a challenging strategy. My goal always is to give you the facts so you can make up your own mind about whether this strategy fits your trading style and personality.

Once again, the last thing I want is for you to lose money. One way to improve your trading skills and reduce mistakes is to use a simulated trading program. You may want to wait until you succeed in the paper money program before betting real money on day trading strategies.

> **NOTE:** There's so much to say about day trading that I could write a book about it—and in fact, I did: *Start Day Trading Now* (Adams Media) is intended for beginners.

THE PATTERN DAY TRADING RULE

Perhaps the first thing to be aware of is the *pattern day trading rule*, which means that if you have less than $25,000 in your account, you are limited to making only three round-trip day trades within a five-business-day period. If you make that fourth trade, you are designated as a *pattern day trader*. You won't be allowed to trade for 90 days until you have $25,000 in the account.

I know that some traders despise the rule, but it is designed to benefit you. With less than $25,000, beginners are forced to be more selective about their trades. By trading with a small size, you get to improve your trading skills while not risking a large sum of money. Betting too much on one trade has doomed many day traders, a fate I want you to avoid.

Many beginners don't realize that you don't need to invest a lot of money to learn this strategy. It's how you manage your account that determines your success or failure as a trader. The solution: Trade with less money until you gain experience and confidence.

> **HINT:** If you have over $25,000, limit the amount traded in any one position to a percentage that feels right to you, perhaps 5 to 7 percent of your account value, or even as low as 3 percent depending on the size of your portfolio. Active day traders with large accounts may choose to limit their amount traded to only 1 or 2 percent.

THE LIFE OF A DAY TRADER

For many people, it sounds wonderful to be a full-time day trader. You are in control of your time and schedule. You don't have to commute to an office or report to a boss. It's extremely satisfying to make a good trade and be rewarded with money instantly. There's no dress code, and you can set your own financial goals. And don't forget that you can trade from anywhere in the world.

Although it sounds wonderful on paper, day trading is hard work. Without a regular paycheck, many traders feel tremendous pressure to overtrade to make money. You often have to make quick decisions, and the pressure to not lose money is intense. But even with all these challenges, it is possible to be a successful day trader.

The stereotype of a day trader is someone making dozens of lightning-fast trades, risking thousands with the hope of earning $200 to $500. Although some individuals may use this stressful strategy, most modern day traders are more disciplined about their trades. They trade smarter while making only a few transactions in one trading session. The goal is the same—make money in a single day—but how you do it is the key.

DAY TRADING SIGNALS

To succeed as a day trader, rely on the technical indicators introduced in this book. Then adjust the parameters to shorter time frames. It may take some time to find settings that work for you, but be patient.

The sidebar that follows contains some of the signals to look for when using this strategy. Consider them as only guidelines.

DAY TRADING TECHNICAL SIGNALS

- **Moving Averages.** Begin with the 20- and 50-day moving averages (or shorter such as the 10-day) on a 15-minute, 30-minute, or 60-minute chart (some day traders use even shorter time periods). Another choice is the 200-day moving average on a 15-minute chart, which results in fewer signals. There is no right answer of what is best; it's a personal choice.

- **MACD.** For the strongest signals, you want MACD to be above the zero line and above the 9-day signal line. In addition, look for a bullish divergence, as that gives meaningful signals (even if slower than those from stochastics). As a day trader, you can adjust the parameters for faster signals (but not too fast).

- **MACD histogram.** Observe whether the histogram bars are getting darker or lighter, which helps determine if momentum is increasing or decreasing.

- **Slow (or Fast) Stochastics.** Watch for %K and %D to move higher, but if they rise above 75 or 80 (overbought) and cross, it's a sell signal. Day traders have to be extremely careful when stocks get overbought, as reversals are very common.

- **RSI.** Use RSI for intraday overbought or oversold conditions. RSI confirms the strength of the move. If RSI is turning down, then it's possible an overbought stock price is running out of gas. It's not necessarily a sell signal unless it's confirmed with other indicators.

- **Support and resistance.** By now, you know that if a stock breaks below support levels, and the indicators are turning against your position, do not fight the facts. Bail out of the position and consider whether to sell short. Conversely, when a stock price rises above resistance and stays above, and the indicators are on your side, there is no reason to sell at this time.

Ride winning trades as long as you can (this is the artistic part of trading), but think about taking money off the table. Most importantly, sell a winning position before the end of the day. Do the same for a losing position.

- **VWAP (volume weighted average price).** This technical indicator is popular with many day traders. Read the sidebar at the end of this chapter for a detailed discussion on how to use it.

> **HINT:** You cannot control stock prices, but you do have control over the indicators you choose. Use them to guide you into successful trades.

· · · · · · · · ·

While it's easy for me to tell you when to buy and sell based on the above indicators, the challenge of day trading is that everything happens in a flash. That is why a trade plan is so essential for day traders. This helps you identify appropriate entry and exit prices. This is not the kind of strategy where you can "wing it" (trade without a plan).

Most importantly, do not violate the number one rule for day traders: Do not hold overnight! Many beginners enter a day trade with every intention of selling by the end of the day. Later, when the position runs into trouble, they override the indicators and their rules with a hunch that tomorrow will be better.

It doesn't matter whether they exited profitably the following day. They broke their own rules. Once you break your rules, the consequences are often severe.

> **THE BOTTOM LINE:** Do not forget that you are a day trader. By the end of the day, you must be out of that trade. Break these rules if you must, but if you do, don't call yourself a day trader.

WHAT DAY TRADERS LOOK FOR IN A STOCK

The following are some of the characteristics that day traders desire when searching for winning stocks:

- **Volatile stocks.** Day traders look for stocks that are on the move; that is, they are volatile. The more volatile the stock price, the better it is for most day traders. Why? Because they seek quick profits. Day traders don't have time to buy a slow-moving stock that lingers for days or weeks.
- **High volume.** A key characteristic for a trade candidate is high volume. Some traders won't day-trade stocks with a daily volume less than 400,000 shares (but use your own criteria). Trading higher-volume stocks ensures liquidity, allowing you to easily get into and out of a position. Stocks with low liquidity and low volume are easy to buy, but may be difficult to sell at a price that is good for you.
- **Risk-reward.** Day traders are concerned with risk-reward ratios, and they should be. As you remember, buying a stock that could fall by $1 but has the potential to gain $5 has a risk-reward ratio of 1:5. That is why intraday traders are constantly looking for stocks with excellent risk-reward ratios (at least 1:3).
- **Relative strength.** Many day traders attempt to find stocks that have relative strength. As you may remember from Chapter 1, if the overall market is moving lower but certain stocks on your Watch List are moving higher, then those stocks have relative strength.

  There is no guarantee that these stocks will move higher all day, but for day traders, when these stocks move higher for a few minutes or hours, that's a profitable opportunity.
- **Stock sectors.** Many day traders trade stock *sectors*. For example, instead of buying Microsoft, Alphabet, Adobe, or

Nvidia, day traders may elect to trade the *technology sector* using an ETF. The technology sector ETF (XLK: Technology Select Sector SPDR Fund) is just one of hundreds of stock sectors available.

If the overall market is down, some stock sectors will be up (they have relative strength). For example, if the Dow is falling, you may notice that the pharmaceutical or utility sector is moving higher.

Unfortunately, by the time you discover that a certain sector is strong, it may be too late to buy. As often happens with the market, a sector may begin the day with strength and collapse in the afternoon. That is what makes day-trading sectors a challenging strategy.

HINT: You can use scanning programs to find the strongest sectors each day.

A DAY TRADING STORY

For your education and entertainment, the following is a fictionalized short story about a novice trader, Jerry. I hope that you learn a few lessons from this man's day trading adventure.

After reading a few books about day trading and viewing a couple of online videos, Jerry entered the stock market with a little more than $25,000 in his account. He already knew that he wanted to buy a stock, ZYX, that one of his neighbors recommended.

Jerry didn't look at stock charts or use technical analysis. He just knew that he *must* own this stock right now. As soon as the market opened, Jerry placed a market order to buy 500 shares of ZYX at $18.57 per share at a cost of $9,285.

Only minutes after he bought the stock, the price went a little higher. Jerry watched in delight as the stock jumped by a point a half hour after the opening bell. Unbeknown to Jerry, someone had tweeted that ZYX was going to be bought out by a major manufacturing firm.

Within minutes, Jerry had already made an unrealized gain of $540. Hey, he thought, day trading is easy! He was so excited about his newfound wealth that he shared the news with his sister and tip-giving neighbor. The neighbor told him that he could expect to make a lot more money than that.

Unfortunately, by the time Jerry got off the phone, his $540 gain had turned into a $600 loss. What? Jerry couldn't believe it. Taking his eyes off his trading screen had cost him $1,100. It turned out that the buyout rumor was false.

Jerry decided to try a new strategy, one he had heard about: buying the dip. His neighbor thought the stock was a winner, so Jerry bought an additional 500 shares. He now owned 1,000 shares of ZYX at an average price of $18.01. He was hopeful that the decline was only temporary.

If Jerry had looked at a stock chart, he'd have seen that ZYX was trading below its 20- and 50-day moving averages (breaking support), which scared other investors into selling. MACD had also moved lower, pointing to more pain ahead. Because Jerry didn't use technical analysis, he didn't know any of this.

Once ZYX fell below its moving averages, the algos pounced, selling the stock short with reckless abandon. Within an hour, ZYX plunged to $13.02. When Jerry called his neighbor for advice, his friend said, "It's too cheap to sell. I'm buying more."

Jerry didn't have enough money to buy more shares. He sat glumly in front of the computer and watched his money disappear. His sister called to see how much money he was making, but he told her he was busy.

The only idea Jerry had was to call his friend again.

"Should I sell now?" Jerry asked.

"No!" the neighbor yelled. "Don't be Chicken Little! This stock is going to $50 per share. I've never been more sure about anything in my whole life!"

Jerry had no plan other than doing what his neighbor suggested. Meanwhile, the stock continued to fall until midday when the price moved sideways.

If Jerry had learned more about the stock market before trading, he would have done his "due diligence" rather than rely on stock tips from an unqualified but opinionated neighbor.

After ZYX dropped below its moving averages, Jerry should have stopped adding to the position, and in fact, he should have begun looking to exit. Managing a successful day trade means not only having good judgment but also having the ability to make speedy decisions under stressful conditions when money is on the line.

Jerry made a few more errors before the end of the day. Because ZYX stopped falling, he thought the worst was over. After consulting with his perma-bull neighbor, Jerry decided to hold his position overnight. He hated the idea of losing money.

This turned out to be the worst mistake of all. ZYX was supposed to be a day trade, but Jerry switched strategies based on nothing but hope. He was now a "stuckholder." Unfortunately for Jerry, ZYX dove again after hours, costing Jerry even more money. What were his reasons for holding overnight? His neighbor told him to!

The next day, Jerry wised up and sold his entire position as ZYX continued to fall after the open. He just couldn't take the pain anymore. By the time he sold, he had lost over $8,500.

If he had stayed with the losing trade instead of selling, the losses would have been much greater. What saved Jerry was that he got out of the position the next day.

I don't tell this story to scare you away from day trading. I want to present a small taste of what it's like to lose serious money on a trade. The rewards can be fantastic when you are on the right side of a day trade. However, to achieve success, you must pay your dues—and that usually means losing money as a beginner.

Learning technical analysis is an important first step and one of the reasons I have devoted so much time to these methods. The problem is that many beginners believe that all they have to do is learn technical analysis and they will be successful, but this is not true. It is similar to learning how to use a hammer and saw. Can you build a house just because you know how to use these tools? Of course not. It's the same with day trading.

DAY TRADING HINTS

You just read about an inexperienced trader who stumbled into day trading without a clue of what to do. However, day trading can be a successful strategy if you are disciplined and knowledgeable.

One of the most important characteristics of a successful day trader is patience, contradicting the public's caricature of day traders. You must be certain that the odds of success are in your favor before pressing the Enter key. Always confirm your decision by using the technical tools at your disposal and calculating whether the anticipated reward is worth the risk. Please remember to use a stop-loss order once the trade is made.

Finally, do not trade when you are feeling emotional, rushed, or pressured. That adrenaline rush felt by many traders at the market open leads to poor decision-making and lost money.

Now that you have a better idea of how to succeed as a day trader, the following sidebar tells you how to use a technical indicator favored by many day traders: VWAP.

VOLUME-WEIGHTED AVERAGE PRICE (VWAP)

Imagine that you find a technical indicator used by institutional traders that helps with entering and exiting intraday trades. What if this indicator could let you know whether you were getting a good, bad, or average price?

There is such an indicator: the volume-weighted average price, otherwise known as VWAP. Although it is based on a sophisticated formula, when VWAP is plotted on a chart, it is an uncomplicated, easily decipherable moving average indicator. It is often used by traders who want to get an order filled at a price that is at or near the current VWAP. VWAP also reveals the direction of the current trend. For those reasons (and a few more), it's a mandatory tool for institutions and retail day traders.

VWAP uses a formula based on volume and price to calculate its version of the average stock price over a certain period. To be precise, VWAP is a volume-weighted methodology for determining the average price of the stock over a specific time period, usually one trading day.

When selecting VWAP on any chart program, the plot of the average price appears as a single line on an intraday chart, similar to a moving average. The trader selects an intraday time frame such as 1 minute, 5 minutes, or 15 minutes.

VWAP generates a number of signals. For example, one day trading strategy calls for trading in the direction of the VWAP. If the stock price rises above VWAP, that's bullish. If the stock price drops below VWAP, that's bearish. Many retail day traders also use VWAP to find support and resistance.

In addition, VWAP shows institutional traders (and day traders) whether their purchase price was above or below the daily average price. After all, institutions need to know if they received a price slightly better than VWAP. Their goal is to get the best possible order fill for their large orders (often 500,000 shares and higher). For an institution, those pennies can add up to significant savings.

Here's some advice: If you're a day trader, learn how to use this indicator. VWAP is the tool of choice for institutions, and perhaps now, for you. It can only help your day trading results.

. . . .

As I wrote earlier, of all the high-risk, high-reward strategies in Part Four, day trading is the least risky. You will see what I mean when you read about gap trading, one of the most challenging day trading strategies ever created.

CHAPTER 12

TRADING GAPS

I f you thought that momentum trading was risky, gap trading is like riding a roller coaster without a safety harness. Gap trading is for those who want to take extreme risks for the chance to make higher profits in a short time. This strategy, not recommended for inexperienced traders, is what I call "momentum madness." However, if the idea of trading gaps appeals to you, I urge you to wade carefully through this chapter.

Some traders believe that gap trading is a layup trade that brings easy money. In fact, trading gaps are considered one of the most challenging of all the short-term strategies. It takes a tremendous amount of skill, discipline, and ice-cold emotions to engage in this strategy and exit with a profit. Unfortunately, a lot of amateur traders believe the opposite.

If you are unfamiliar with gaps, the sidebar below includes a brief introduction to the four gap types: *breakaway, runaway* (or *continuation*), *exhaustion*, and *common*.

WHAT ARE GAPS?

Gaps are a common pattern that shows up as blank or open spaces on a chart. It means there was no trading at that price level or price range because the stock price "gapped" (or skipped over) that open space on the chart. You can think of a gap as an empty area where nothing is happening.

When a gap forms, the stock opens *higher* than the previous day's close (*gap up*) or *lower* than the previous day's close (*gap down*). For example, let's say there is breaking news overnight that a pharmaceutical company, ZYX, was approved by the FDA (US Food and Drug Administration) to develop a new flu vaccine.

When the news is announced after the close of trading, buyers overwhelm sellers in after-hours selling. The previous close of ZYX was $66 per share. Now, ZYX is spiking higher. In the premarket, ZYX is trading for $72 per share.

As soon as the stock begins trading (and it's likely to have a delayed opening due to an order imbalance), the stock price of ZYX gaps from its previous close of $66 to an astonishing $74 per share. When you look at a stock chart, there is a gap between $66 and $74 where no shares have been traded. There was an order imbalance between buyers and sellers (that is, supply was dwarfed by demand) resulting in the large gap on a stock chart. After a gap has occurred, there is usually extraordinary volume, either intense buying (gap up) or selling (gap down).

Breakaway Gap

The example above describes the *breakaway gap*, which not only is the most exciting, but brings the most profits when the trade works. This gap type occurs early in the trend when a stock moves higher on greater-than-average volume.

Some traders attempt to buy a breakaway gap right at the open (usually while the stock price is consolidating). It takes a lot of practice to enter and exit a gap at the right time, as well as excellent risk management skills.

Runaway (or Continuation) Gap

Many beginners confuse the *runaway gap* with the breakaway gap, and it's easy to see why. At first glance, they seem similar because both involve a move higher, above resistance, or a break below support (if shorting). However, there are subtle differences.

With a runaway gap, the stock is already moving in a certain direction (up or down) when the price jumps higher or lower for whatever reason. Basically, the price continues in the same direction but with more power behind it. It is a continuation of the trend.

HINT: Runaway gaps appear less frequently than breakaway gaps.

Exhaustion Gap

The exhaustion gap occurs when a stock has made a move higher on less-than-normal volume and runs out of steam as demand for the stock declines. With little volume or enthusiasm, the stock price falters rather rapidly.

Exhaustion gaps are characteristically followed by a noticeable reversal, which often incites a mad dash out of the stock (triggering a flood of sell orders). Volume may increase as the exhausted stock retreats and once bullish buyers turn into bearish sellers.

Some contrarian traders like to trade exhaustion gaps. The stock makes an extremely strong move that may play out over one or two days but eventually runs out of energy and stalls. There just aren't enough eager buyers to propel the stock higher or enough sellers to push it much lower. This type of gap often signifies a trend change.

Exhaustion gap is a perfect description: The stock is tired, or "exhausted," and is ready to reverse direction. The exhaustion gap is the clue that "something" has changed. If it is a true exhaustion gap, the stock will continue moving in the opposite direction, and may even *fill the gap* (return to the pre-gap price).

Common Gaps

The gap that appears most often on a chart is the appropriately named *common gap*. For example, if there is a gap between the closing and opening prices, the amount is so small that it's insignificant, maybe only a few pennies. For instance, you look on a chart and notice there is a gap between the $60 close and the opening price of $60.10. Common gaps don't usually provide trading opportunities.

Now that you have an overall picture of the main gap types, let's continue our discussion on how to profit from them. As you may have guessed, the breakaway gap is the riskiest because a sudden reversal can be costly. However, if your timing is accurate, it can also bring the most profits.

NOTE: The remainder of this chapter is devoted only to trading the breakaway gap.

. . . .

TRADING THE BREAKAWAY GAP

When trading a breakaway gap, traders can make tremendous profits when on the right side of a trade. However, if you are on the wrong side, it can "rip your face off," as traders sometimes quip.

HINT: An intelligent stop-loss order protects your account and your face.

A breakaway gap indicates that something so dramatic happened that supply and demand got distorted. This unexpected event results in a significant price gap between the previous day's closing and the next day's opening prices.

There are a dozen reasons why there is a wide gap. If it's a *breakout*, it could be news about a drug being approved by the FDA, a rumor of a takeover, or a positive earnings surprise. If it's a *breakdown*, it could be an accounting investigation or a negative earnings surprise.

The reasons why a stock gapped up or down aren't important to professional traders. In fact, the "why" is almost always irrelevant to them. Think like a pro and focus on "what" is happening to the stock price.

If you step into this volatile, fast-moving trade, you'd better know what you're doing, and that means having strict price controls (including mental stops, where appropriate). Not only does the price gap by a large amount, but volatility increases.

There should also be a jump in volume. On a normal day, perhaps the volume is no more than 1 million shares. After the opening, don't be surprised to see volume zoom to 10 million or 20 million shares or more.

That volume increase is likely because of institutional investors, who cannot be ignored. Plenty of short-term traders also want in on the action. That is why a gapping stock can be profitable for day traders as well as swing, overnight, and weekly traders. The strategy involves buying in an uptrend or shorting into a downtrend. Selecting a good entry point is crucial.

Figure 12.1 is an example of a stock gapping up at the open.

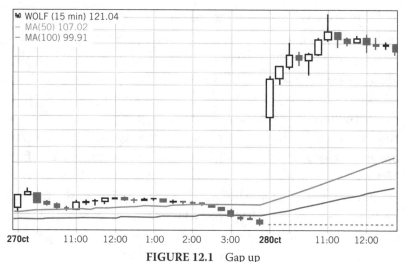

FIGURE 12.1 Gap up
(Chart courtesy of StockCharts.com.)

NEVER DIVE INTO A GAP

One important lesson: Don't impulsively dive into a stock just because its price has gapped up or down. That is simply too risky—similar to jumping off the side of a mountain into a small pond.

If you recklessly trade on the wrong side of a breakaway gap, the financial pain can be excruciating. It could take weeks or months to recover from your losses if you fail to manage this trade properly. If you are an impatient trader who trades breakaway gaps without a plan, there is a high likelihood you're going to lose money.

Preventing a large loss should be your primary objective as a trader. Profits take care of themselves, but losses never do. Proceed with caution when trading gaps.

The following sidebar presents a few of the technical signals to look for when using this strategy.

GAP TRADING TECHNICAL SIGNALS

- **Moving averages.** You are looking for stocks to rise substantially above their 20-, 50-, and 100-day moving averages.

- **MACD.** You want momentum to be on your side (MACD must be above the zero line and above the 9-day signal line). However, be alert to a bearish divergence; that is, the stock moves higher while MACD moves lower. It is a red flag when the stock price moves in the opposite direction of the indicator.

- **MACD histogram.** As a gap trader, you want the bars to get darker, a signal that momentum is increasing. Don't forget that momentum moves before prices, so be ready to abandon your position if momentum weakens.

- **Slow Stochastic.** You want %K and %D moving higher. However, if they move above 75 or 80 (overbought) and cross, that is a sell signal. Gap traders must be extremely careful when stocks get overbought, as reversals are very common.

- **RSI.** Use RSI to identify overbought conditions and confirm the strength of the uptrend. If RSI suddenly turns lower, it's possible the stock price is building downside momentum. It's not necessarily a sell signal, but it's wise to confirm with other indicators. As a gap trader, you can't hold an overbought position very long. You don't want to be trapped in a long position when it reverses.

  Note that when RSI is 90 or higher or 15 or less, that is a clue that the stock price has been pushed to extreme overbought or oversold conditions. Of course, prices can become more extreme, but at this point you are playing with fire.

- **Volatility.** If volatility is expanding, that is a positive sign for gap traders. This often occurs when overbought stocks gap even higher. The first red flag is when momentum begins to contract.

- **Support and resistance.** You want the stock price to break above support or break through resistance, and other indicators to turn positive. As a gap trader, ride the short-term uptrend as long as you can, but be very cautious. Every gap trader has his or her own selling criteria, but even if the stock is well above support, you may want to look for an exit point.

•   **Candlesticks**. The candlesticks are going to turn green when the stock gaps higher. However, look for a series of red candlesticks, a sign the gapped stock may have stalled.

· · · · · · · · ·

HINT: It is recommended that you practice in a simulated trading program or trade small when using this strategy. Also, look for extreme price discrepancies in the futures market (such as a stock price up by 10 or 15 percent from its closing price in the premarket).

DON'T TRADE IN THE FIRST FIVE MINUTES

As we discussed in an earlier chapter, some novice traders are so excited about making money that they rush into a trade in the first five minutes after the market opens. That is when all overnight and new market orders from eager investors reacting to breaking news are set to be filled. It's better to stay away from those first few minutes and let the bulls and bears fight it out without you.

NOTE: As with momentum stocks, the number one rule for gap traders is not to chase. If you missed the move, wait for a better opportunity or change strategies.

WHEN TO SELL

Another difficulty with trading gaps is timing the exit. It's true that you can make educated guesses using technical analysis. Oscillators are especially useful in identifying overbought or oversold conditions. Nevertheless, you must interpret the data correctly and act (hold or exit) quickly.

Unfortunately, when a stock gaps, the duration of the trend is unknowable (even more so than with other types of price trends). Often, it appears more like a guessing game. Without specific reference points, it's similar to trading as if you were floating in outer space.

In reality, it takes tremendous discipline to sell when profits are peaking, but that's exactly what experienced gap traders must do. If they get too fearful or greedy about a stock position, their account may suffer. Using this strategy requires nerves of steel.

WHEN GAP TRADES GO WRONG

When the energy that fuels momentum stocks ends, it can get ugly very fast. Sometimes gapping stocks abruptly reverse direction by retracing 38.2 or 61.8 percent (these are *Fibonacci* retracement levels that are often used for support and resistance). In addition, applying Newton's third law of motion, the sharper the move to the upside, the sharper the reversal may be to the downside.

If trapped in a losing position, the only solution is to get out at the first opportunity. It doesn't mean to sell in a panic along with everyone else, but it does mean to find a reasonable time and price to get out.

Don't take it personally when you lose money on a reversal (or on any trade). When trading stocks like these, reversals are unpredictable. There is nothing to do but cut your losses and exit. Figure out what went wrong and try to do better the next time.

Here's some advice: Often the best strategy is not trading a breakaway gap. It is only for those who not only love risk but know how to manage it.

TESLA: A GAP TRADER'S DREAM STOCK

For a time, the gap trader's dream stock was Tesla—where big money could be made and lost before midday. On some days, Tesla's stock opened higher by 8 percent or more and ended the day up by over 15 percent. If you were on the right side, the gains were fantastic.

If wrong, your account could have been damaged (my hope is that you are not trading gap stocks on margin, or the percentage loss will substantially increase). Obviously, Tesla will not always be a gap trader's dream stock, even though it was in the past. In fact, by the time you're reading this, Tesla may have lost some of its momo.

If so, there will always be other securities to take its place. For example, at the time of this writing, bitcoin continues to make extreme moves on certain days, and that may continue. Fast-moving stocks like these don't come around that often, but when they do, money can be made and lost in a flash.

NOTORIOUSLY UNPREDICTABLE

By now, I hope that you realize that trading gaps is an extremely challenging strategy. Stocks that began the day gapping higher or lower are notoriously unpredictable and volatile, so use this strategy with your eyes wide open. It takes tremendous discipline and focus to be a successful gap trader.

FADING THE GAP: HIGHER RISK, HIGHER REWARD

There are a few brave traders who thrive on a volatile and fast-moving countertrend strategy called *fading the gap*. It simply means trading in the opposite direction of the gap. The pros who use this strategy may be in and out of the trade within minutes, even seconds. They take advantage of price discrepancies in the first five or ten minutes after the market opens, during amateur hour.

Fading the gap is for the most disciplined and fearless traders who are religious about containing risk. If you get on the wrong side of one of these trades, it can wreak havoc with your emotions and account.

One thing is certain: It is difficult to consistently get on the right side when fading gaps. Don't try this strategy with the "eye test," a hunch, or your gut, because it is doubtful it will end well. This strategy rightfully belongs in the high-risk, high-reward category.

Most importantly, do not place big bets when fading the gap. You could make money five times in a row, but on the sixth trade, a month's worth of trading profits could be wiped out. One of my friends calls this a "rolling the dice" trade, and he's right. You never know how this unpredictable trade will turn out.

As with any other gap or momentum strategies, fade the gap with only one stock at a time, and trade small. As always, practice this strategy in a simulated account before trading in the live account.

Now that you know how to make or lose money trading gaps, for your entertainment and education, I want to tell you a true story of what happened to an investor friend of mine, David (not his real name). Unfortunately, he inadvertently got caught in a breakaway gap.

ANALYSIS: TRUE STORY OF A BREAKAWAY GAP DISASTER

A few years ago, David and a few friends bought shares of Athenex, Inc. (symbol: ATNX), a global biopharmaceutical company, as a long-term investment. He and his buddies created an informal investment group focused on this one stock. After talking with his friends, David made a lump-sum investment of $153,000 for 17,000 shares of Athenex at $9 per share.

For years, these buddies stuck with the stock, riding it higher, cheering it on as if it were their favorite sports team. Not surprisingly, they urged each other to buy even more shares on every dip—and there were many dips on the way up.

Everything went swimmingly for several years. David and the others in his one-stock investment club amassed huge unrealized profits as Athenex climbed from $9 to $20 per share in 2020.

Then something unexpected happened. On March 1, 2021, during the after-hours market, Athenex started to sell off strongly. According to overnight news reports, the FDA had expressed concerns about a breast cancer drug that the company had developed. The FDA said the drug was not ready for approval at this time.

When Athenex opened for trading the next morning, it had gapped *down* to less than $6 per share, a 55 percent haircut and a perfect example of a breakaway gap. Anyone who held shares in this company, including David, woke up with indigestion.

How do you trade a frightening gap? The first thing is not to panic, admittedly not easy to do when losses are accumulating. After the gap down, Athenex was obviously below its 50-, 100-, and 200-day moving averages on extremely high volume.

Indicators such as MACD signaled that this stock was in deep trouble. The only indicator that gave hope to bullish investors was RSI, which dropped to near 10, reflecting severe oversold conditions.

Figure 12.2 displays a screenshot of ATNX on the day it gapped down.

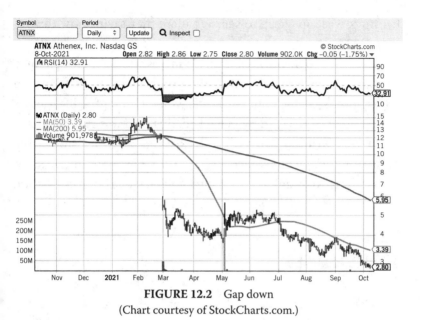

FIGURE 12.2 Gap down
(Chart courtesy of StockCharts.com.)

• • • • • • • •

HOW TO TRADE A STOCK THAT GAPPED DOWN

In hindsight, anyone holding Athenex should have made plans to sell the entire position. Many investors didn't do that because they were true believers, high on "hopium." Wise traders and investors don't argue with the tape—they cut their losses promptly. The reason why Athenex fell is irrelevant—only that it did. The only proper action is to sell the shares and deploy the cash to a more favorable candidate.

Here's how this sad story ended: Weeks later, Athenex gapped down a second time to $4 per share. The stock didn't recover from the second shellacking, and in fact, was trading at less than $3 per share several months later, eventually reaching penny stock status. Those who held shares at $6 might have convinced themselves that this stock was too cheap to sell. What are they saying now that it's under $3?

According to David, he sold all his shares after the stock plunged to near $6. However, several of the group members who owned shares never sold, including one man who put his entire life savings into the stock. The last time I checked, this man was still holding.

At this writing, Athenex still exists as a penny stock. The chances of a miraculous recovery are slim, but more importantly, the last thing you want to be is a stuckholder. Hope is never a reason to hold a stock.

LESSONS LEARNED

Had David followed technical indicators, he might have detected signs of trouble long before Athenex gapped down that day. When this stock had reached all-time highs at $20, it repelled hard, sinking below its moving averages to $15 per share before finding support. Clearly, it hit resistance at $20, a warning sign.

An astute trader might have sold at $15 per share, especially when this stock had fallen below its moving averages. Although technical indicators can't forecast the future, they did a good job of alerting him of the risks.

I also understand why David didn't sell at that time. After all, Athenex had reversed direction many times in the past. Each time investors bought the dip previously, they were rewarded.

Besides relying too much on dip buying, David made another huge psychological error: He and his friends fell in love with the company and its stock. Once they became cheerleaders, they lost their objectivity. They wouldn't dare sell a stock they perceived as family. Even more perilous, many in the group held an unusually large number of shares of this microcap stock.

I have seen this happen with other investors. Instead of diversifying into other investments, or investing less money, they bet it all on one of their darlings. These investors usually get wiped out during a correction or crash.

It's true that if the drug had been approved, David and his buddies would have looked like geniuses. That's what David missed: This investment was a gamble, an all-or-nothing trade. As traders, we should not get involved with all-or-nothing trades. That's not trading—that's a wildly speculative crapshoot.

Although no one could have predicted that Athenex would gap down on a particular day, once it happened, it was time to sell and get out. The stock was so broken, it may take years to recover.

David waited a couple of days before selling. When Athenex didn't bounce back immediately, he claimed that he sold his entire position. Instead of locking in a $187,000 profit, he lost approximately $51,000. If he had not sold when he did, he would have lost another $50,000.

· · · · · · · ·

If you thought trading gaps was exciting (or terrifying if you are risk-averse), then you may love the next chapter on trading cryptocurrencies. Cryptocurrency trading is more speculation than investing, but because so many readers are fascinated by this product, I felt compelled to include it. Love it or hate it, cryptocurrencies are here to stay.

I'll do my best to explain how cryptocurrencies work, and how to make a profit trading them.

CHAPTER 13

CRYPTOCURRENCIES

M y first introduction to cryptocurrencies was in 2015 when my neighbor Leo told me about the first digital currency, bitcoin, which was selling for $300 per coin. I was intrigued but confused by the idea of a currency that exists only on a computer.

Leo explained that the currency was stored on the computer in digital format. He made a bold prediction: "One day bitcoin will be worth $50,000 each."

I scoffed at his prediction. "You think so?" I asked skeptically. Obviously, I didn't believe him or his wild theories.

I did a little research on the technology but felt it was too speculative for my tastes, so I passed on buying even one coin. Nevertheless, Leo was obsessed with cryptocurrencies, and we had numerous conversations about this new technology. He showed me his account and explained how to make trades.

When bitcoin hit $3,000 per coin a few years later, Leo couldn't help himself. He called me to say that he paid $60,000 for 20 bitcoins, all the money that he had. Again, I passed on the idea. I know not to listen to investment ideas from neighbors or friends. Later, I will tell you what happened to Leo and his 20 bitcoins.

As for me, if I had followed his early advice (one of the rare times a neighbor was right about an investment) and plunged into bitcoin, I'd be writing this book in my luxury yacht off the coast of France.

In this chapter, I introduce you to cryptocurrencies, the technology that makes them work, and their risks and rewards. Love them or hate them, cryptocurrencies will be in the news for a very long time.

CRYPTOCURRENCY BASICS

A cryptocurrency is a digital currency that exists only in electronic format, a reason it is called *digital gold* or *electronic money*. The confusing part for many people is that it was created by computer code (*crypto*). Cryptocurrency can be used as a form of payment to buy goods or services by anyone who accepts that specific currency.

The revolutionary idea behind crypto is this: While the dollar, euro, peso, krone, krona, and yen are all backed by a government, crypto was purposely created so that no individual entity is regulating or controlling the currency. It is a decentralized technology that is spread out among thousands of computers that record and manage the transactions.

The technology that makes cryptocurrency work is *blockchain*, a data storage program that contains and tracks every transaction—linked together using all the computers in the network (on the blockchain). It uses encrypted computer code called *cryptography*.

Blockchain was designed to make it difficult to cheat the system. It is supposed to be "unhackable" although there have been a few breaches (when hackers overrode the blockchain protocols).

The blockchain is a public list of every cryptocurrency transaction and address, one of the ways to "vet" crypto transactions and avoid duplications. The blockchain ledger makes it easier to keep track of trades.

Blockchain technology makes it possible for crypto to exist without support from a government or bank. This means that a central bank or government is not allowed to "dilute" the value of the currency by printing more of it. This is one of many reasons why cryptocurrencies have become so valuable. It is also why many governments abhor them; cryptocurrencies were designed to avoid government regulation.

STORING CRYPTO

Because there is no physical bill or coin to hold in your hand, cryptocurrencies are stored in an electronic device (such as a computer, online, external hard drive, or *digital wallet*) with a digital or *private key* (a password).

The only way to gain access to your cryptocurrency funds is with a *crypto wallet address*, that is, a long and unique string of characters. With that address, you can convert the crypto to cash and eventually move it to a bank account. Accessing the wallet is also how you send and receive cryptocurrencies. It goes without saying that you had better not forget your crypto address, or your private key.

TYPES OF CRYPTOCURRENCIES

The most well-known and largest cryptocurrencies are bitcoin and Ethereum, but there are thousands more, and new currencies are constantly being created through an elaborate process called *mining*. In fact, some people accumulate cryptocurrencies by mining, which involves tedious mathematical equations.

> **ADVICE:** Although there are thousands of cryptocurrencies (some real, some fake), stick with the most popular and most liquid crypto in the world: bitcoin. After you gain more experience, feel free to trade other currencies. But you have to start somewhere, so start by trading bitcoin. (After bitcoin, Ethereum is the second largest currency.)

WHY CENTRAL BANKS DISLIKE CRYPTOCURRENCIES

If you think that cryptocurrencies frighten most central banks, you are right. In essence, cryptocurrencies are "stateless" with no connection to a government or financial institution. A vast group of computers control the digital asset.

People in some countries, especially those who live under authoritarian governments, can use cryptocurrency to move money around the globe without government restrictions. It's also easy for criminals to move money to different countries without detection, a thorn in the side of law enforcement.

Although some governments are threatened by cryptocurrencies, not all believe it's a bad idea. For example, El Salvador was the first country to make cryptocurrency legal tender. Going forward, some central banks will create their own version of digital currencies. As they say, if you can't beat them, join them.

THE BENEFITS

The positive aspect of cryptocurrencies is that without an intermediary such as a central bank, no one can make the price of crypto move up or down. It moves based on true supply and demand.

The biggest fans believe that crypto will eventually replace traditional currencies such as the dollar, euro, or yen. In fact, many Wall Street firms have been investing heavily in cryptocurrencies, one of the reasons cryptocurrencies such as bitcoin have skyrocketed in value.

In addition, companies such as Microsoft, AT&T, and Mastercard allow customers to pay in cryptocurrency, and more will follow. With support by institutions and corporations, it is hard for critics to dismiss crypto as only a fad (perhaps these were the same critics that proclaimed the internet would not last the summer).

THE RISKS

Because cryptocurrencies are not backed by a financial entity, if your cryptocurrency is hacked or if you send bitcoin to the wrong person, there is no way to get a refund. That is one of several reasons why cryptocurrencies are so risky.

Many traditional investors can't stand the idea of cryptocurrencies. For example, at a 2021 shareholder meeting, Berkshire Hathaway vice chairman Charlie Munger said that bitcoin was nothing more than "artificial gold" that was "contrary to the interests of civilization."

There are other risks. For example, if the online crypto exchange company that handles your transaction goes out of business or is hacked, or if you lose your password or your digital wallet is stolen, your money has vanished. There is no customer service phone number to help retrieve your money, another reason to protect your private key.

The most common problem is sending the currency to the wrong person. If the recipient does not agree to return the crypto, there's no way to reverse the transaction. Scammers insist on being paid in crypto for that reason.

> **HINT:** If someone refuses to accept forms of payment other than crypto, that is a red flag.

WHERE TO STORE CRYPTO

As mentioned earlier, because the currency exists only as computer code, it's essential that cryptocurrencies are stored in a digital wallet—preferably offline on a computer, thumb drive, or mobile device.

Another choice is to simply leave your cryptocurrency with a cryptocurrency exchange where you can trade hundreds of different digital currencies including bitcoin. The largest platform at the time of this writing is Coinbase. There are other exchanges that you can use, but that's the most well known. You can always switch your account to other trading platforms.

In the future, other firms will offer custodial services for cryptocurrency traders. For example, in 2022 State Street Corporation partnered with Copper.co to hold digital assets for institutional clients in a digital wallet.

CRYPTO SCAMS

The worst part of engaging with this product is that the crypto universe is populated with manipulators and pump-and-dumpers who give misleading advice on social media, lure you into buying their bogus currencies, or try to convince you to join their phony crypto exchanges. Right now, crypto is a speculative investment, and if you have done your research, you should be able to avoid the most blatant scams.

Most importantly, avoid fancy-looking crypto exchanges that you have never heard anything about. Many are fly-by-night scam sites designed to take your money. Do some basic research, and never give your money to unknown companies. Another problem: Many smaller exchanges are susceptible to getting hacked.

HISTORY

The first cryptocurrency, bitcoin, was introduced in a white paper in 2008 titled: "Bitcoin: A Peer-to-Peer Electronic Cash System." The paper, authored by Satoshi Nakamoto (a pseudonym), was published one month after Lehman Brothers collapsed during the sub-prime mortgage crisis.

One year later, Nakamoto created the first blockchain database. The true identify of this person or group has never been revealed. Nakamoto vanished in 2010 and hasn't been heard from since.

On May 22, 2010, the first cryptocurrency transaction occurred when a Florida man, Laszlo Hanyecz, bought two pizzas with 10,000 bitcoins. At the time, these bitcoins were worth only four-tenths of one cent apiece (totaling approximately $40). Every year, crypto fans around the world celebrate May 22 as Bitcoin Pizza Day.

CRYPTOCURRENCY'S FUTURE

Many people want to know if cryptocurrencies are a scam, the wave of the future, or a huge bubble that will pop one day. Unless you are a fortune-teller, no one knows, but the hope of crypto proponents is that paying with crypto currency someday will be as common as paying with cash or a credit card.

No matter what you think about crypto, owning this currency is akin to taking a wild roller coaster ride at a theme park. That is why cryptocurrency traders often tell each other that if they want to survive, they'd better HODL (hold on for dear life). If you can stomach the steep declines, volatility, and random price spikes, the return can be very rewarding (or devastating).

NOTE: A popular resource for bitcoin traders is TradingView (www.tradingview.com).

Non-fungible Tokens

Many unique digital products are being developed including *non-fungible tokens* (NFTs). Technically, NFTs are stored on an

Ethereum blockchain (although some are held on another block-chain network, Binance Smart Chain [BSC]). The word *non-fungible* is another way of saying they are unique and irreplaceable. Think of an NFT as a "smart" contract that certifies or verifies ownership of a digital asset.

NFTs have exploded in popularity, and many people don't know why. In particular, they have shocked the art world, where digital art NFTs have sold for hundreds of thousands and even millions of dollars.

Here's what many people don't understand: Some NFT investors are paying big bucks to own something that can be viewed online by anyone. As a buyer of an NFT digital image, for example, the block-chain ledger is your proof that you own a unique token on the block-chain. If the value increases, you can sell it to someone else for a higher price. Or you can keep the digital art knowing you are its true owner.

In the future, NFTs will move from the art world to games, music, film, and numerous other new media. The surge in interest in NFTs will likely continue, but like anything connected to digital transactions, their future is unknown.

CAN YOU MAKE MONEY TRADING CRYPTO?

Some people believe that cryptocurrencies are a good long-term investment, while others consider them only for speculation. No one can say which method is best.

The first question most beginners want to know is, "Can I make money trading crypto?" The answer is yes, but it takes skill, discipline, and due diligence. Crypto is still in its early stages, and it may take years for it to be accepted and backed by most governments or institutions. Until then, buyer beware.

To buy or sell cryptocurrencies, you may open an account at an online cryptocurrency exchange company. As mentioned earlier, the largest cryptocurrency company to go public on the US stock market is Coinbase. Keep in mind that you don't have to go through an exchange to trade cryptocurrencies, but many people do because it is convenient.

The second question beginners usually ask is, "Is this the right time to buy cryptocurrencies?" The answer is simple: No one knows.

Like any new technology, the value of crypto cannot be determined by traditional methods. This is what upsets investors like Charlie Munger. Still, fear of the unknown hasn't stopped institutional investors from piling into cryptocurrencies and profiting from their meteoric rise.

In my opinion, although cryptocurrencies are still in the early stages, if some of the security kinks can be solved, and if legal protections are included, then buying with crypto will eventually be accepted by the public.

Option contracts had a similar problem in their early years. In fact, it took more than 100 years for options to become standardized and accepted by the general public. Perhaps crypto will take a similar route.

Until more rules are established and there is more accountability, trading crypto is still too volatile for most investors. I believe the future is bright for cryptocurrencies, but it is still too early for them to replace traditional currencies.

MY NEIGHBOR LEO

I wanted to tell you what happened to my neighbor Leo and his 20 bitcoins. He held on for dear life as the value of his coins climbed higher (with numerous twists and turns along the way). Then one day, bitcoin spiked to $20,000 per coin. On that day, Leo had a $340,000 gain.

He called me on the phone that day to tell me the good news. "I'm going to buy a Lamborghini or a new house," he rejoiced. I could hear the euphoria in his voice.

When I suggested that he sell a couple of coins, he scoffed. "It's going to $100,000 per coin," he predicted, double his initial prediction.

A few weeks after this conversation, bitcoin plunged from $20,000 down to $6,000. Leo sold in a panic as bitcoin fell, selling at lower prices, but still squeaking out a small gain.

A few months later, he sold his house, and I haven't heard from him since. I have no idea what happened to him, and whether he continued to hold on for dear life. If he had held onto his original 20 coins, his gain would have been $1,140,000 when bitcoin went as high as $60,000 per coin. Perhaps Leo's prediction of $100,000 will yet come true.

I thought a long time about bitcoin and Leo's trading experiences. Although his original prediction was on target, he succumbed to his emotions when bitcoin plunged. I learned from observing Leo that money can be made and lost trading this product, but it is a challenging endeavor.

BEFORE TRADING

If you are determined to trade cryptocurrencies (or any other financial product), do your due diligence. After all, it takes time to find a reliable cryptocurrency to buy.

Don't be in a rush to buy crypto for the same reasons that you don't rush in to buy stocks. Just like the stock market, the crypto market will still be there when you decide to participate.

For now, take the time to get a crypto education. After you have assessed the benefits and risks and found a cryptocurrency that's worth owning, only then should you consider participating in this market.

NOTE: If you want to learn more about cryptocurrencies as well as other high-risk, high-reward products such as NFTs, read *A Beginner's Guide to High-Risk, High-Reward Investing* by Robert Ross (Adams Media). As well, there are many other books about cryptocurrencies online and at bookstores.

. . . .

If you are looking for other speculative investments, one popular but risky idea is to trade penny stocks, or stocks that are selling for under $5 per share. These are stocks in companies that were unable to make it to the major exchanges.

Although the "pennies" appear cheap, it's easy to lose money trading these products since almost all of them are long shots. A lot of people are interested in trading the pennies, one of the reasons I included them in the next chapter. Although not for everyone (or even for most people), it's worth your time to learn how they work.

CHAPTER 14

PENNY STOCKS

This chapter introduces a popular high-risk strategy: buying penny stocks. As always, I will do my best to tell you the facts about this strategy so you know the risks and rewards. While some traders have been successful with trading penny stocks, many have not.

If you were thinking of trading penny stocks, please read this entire chapter first. (That crying sound you hear is from the rookies who are bleeding money because they had bought these products with no clue of what they were doing. I am here to help prevent the tears and the bloodshed.)

TRADING PENNY STOCKS

Penny stocks trade for less than $5 per share according to the SEC (Securities and Exchange Commission). Because the stocks of these small corporations don't meet the minimum requirements for listing on a major stock exchange, they trade over the counter (OTC) on the Nasdaq. They are called *pink sheet* stocks because the names and prices of these stocks were once printed on pink paper.

People trade penny stocks because the extremely low share price is so affordable. There is always the hope that one of the "pennies" will double and redouble, making traders big returns on a small investment.

For example, for only $1,000 you can buy 2,000 shares of a penny stock at $0.50 per share. If the stock ever makes it to a dollar, the profit would be 100 percent ($1,000 in this example). That is the lure of penny stocks, but the low price is usually an illusion.

Let me explain: You could buy a penny stock for $1.00 and watch it drop to $0.70 within days (or even the same day). This happens all the time with the pennies. Penny stocks are cheap for a reason. It could be that they are the stocks of companies that are poorly managed, have little or no earnings, or have too much debt. Whatever the cause, there aren't enough buyers to push the stocks higher.

Even with their low price, there is usually not much interest in these stocks. Therefore, trading *volume* is exceptionally low. For example, most stocks on the major stock exchanges trade millions of shares every day, whereas a penny stock may trade no more than 10,000 shares per day, and often even less.

A number of traders specialize in these stocks, although succeeding using penny stock strategies requires discipline, knowledge, superb timing skills, and luck. Another huge problem with trading penny stocks is that the price is easy to manipulate. Because of the low volume, manipulation happens often with the pennies.

For example, if someone enters to buy 10,000 shares of a $1 stock trading only 25,000 shares a day, the trade will affect the price. That's also why some people with lots of money trade penny stocks: They can influence the price of these low-priced stocks. After the price spikes because of a large buy order, they sell their shares, leaving everyone else in the dust. The price plummets before existing investors can get out.

I know that some of you may rationalize the money that you're spending on penny stocks by saying to yourself, "It only costs $1,000, but I could make $10,000!" The cold hard truth is it's very rare to hit a home run with a penny stock.

IF YOU INSIST ON TRADING PENNY STOCKS

Even with the risks, there are a few ways to successfully trade the pennies, but it isn't easy; instead of making home runs, most strike out. Although the low cost is alluring, do not attempt to buy penny stocks to "get rich quick." It rarely happens.

If you are one of the rare individuals who can make a profit by trading penny stocks, or are determined to succeed, here are a few guidelines:

- Find stocks that have strong-looking charts (e.g., the technical indicators and oscillators are bullish).
- If you do make a 20 or 30 percent return, take the money and run. In the penny stock world, that 30 percent gain could evaporate quickly.
- Pick penny stocks that trade at least 100,000 shares per day. As I've mentioned, penny stocks with low volume and liquidity are easily manipulated.
- Use only limit orders with penny stocks, never market orders. Penny stocks are cheap for a reason, so trade cautiously.
- Trade with a small amount of money, as it's easy to lose it all.

NOTE: The website that discusses the rules and offers other information about the over-the-counter stocks is www.otcbb.com, a "bulletin board" managed by FINRA (Financial Industry Regulatory Authority) and used by FINRA subscribers. If you're not a subscriber, click on the magnifying glass and search for "over-the-counter stocks" or "penny stocks." Information about these stocks will be displayed.

SUGGESTION: Before trading the pennies, be sure to compose a list of rules of when to buy and when to sell. Penny stock traders must be disciplined, and that means following your rules.

PENNY STOCK TRADING SIGNALS

You should know that because of low liquidity and weak trading volume, technical indicators don't work consistently with penny stocks, and often not at all. Some penny stock traders have turned to fundamental analysis for answers. Learning everything you can about the company before buying its stock is a wise move.

With those caveats, here are a few of the technical indicators to look for when trading the pennies:

- **Moving averages.** You are looking for penny stocks to break above their 20-, 50-, and 100-day moving averages.
- **MACD.** You want momentum to be on your side (MACD must be above the zero line and above the 9-day signal line). Some traders say MACD is one of the most reliable indicators for penny stocks.
- **MACD histogram.** Look for the bars to get darker, a signal that momentum is increasing. As a penny stock trader, you want to see momentum strengthen. Don't forget that momentum moves before prices, so be ready to abandon your position if momentum weakens.
- **RSI.** Use RSI to identify overbought conditions and to confirm the strength of the uptrend. If RSI suddenly turns lower, it's possible the stock price is building downside momentum. It's not necessarily a sell signal, but it's wise to confirm by using other indicators. As a penny stock trader, you can't hold an overbought penny stock for very long or you'll be trapped on the wrong side of a long position.
- **Volatility.** If volatility expands, that is a positive sign for penny stocks. This often occurs when overbought stocks are spiking higher. Most importantly, don't overstay your visit at the penny party or you may get trapped. The first sign of trouble is when momentum begins to contract. That is a red flag.

- **Support and resistance.** You are on the right side if you are long when the penny stock breaks above resistance. As a trader, ride the uptrend as long as you can, but be cautious. Even if the stock breaks above resistance, you may want to look for an exit strategy. Each penny stock trader has their own selling criteria, so use whatever works.

. . . .

Although some of the technical indicators above should help if you trade penny stocks, before you go, I want to alert you to the most common penny stock schemes, scams, and risks.

PENNY STOCK RISKS

If you are tempted to trade the pennies because they are affordable, I'm going to walk you through some of the risks. Please read about the things that can go wrong before making your first live trade.

These microcap stocks are on the pink sheets for a reason, and it's not because these companies have great earnings, or any earnings. Perhaps they were once good companies that lost their way, or they are terrible companies with little or no earnings. There are no minimum standards for pink sheet stocks, so it's possible you are buying worthless junk.

> **NOTE:** The odds are extremely high that most of the penny stocks listed in the pink sheets will fail. However, one of the very few companies that actually recovered from penny stock status was Apple. Most agree those were one-in-a-million odds, and the resurgence was thanks to the genius of Steve Jobs. Don't expect that your penny stock will be like Apple. These stocks are in the basement for a reason.

PENNY STOCK SCAMS

Because of their low volume but high volatility, penny stocks are often used by unethical people to hook you into buying cheap but nearly worthless stocks. They call you on the phone or send phishing emails or texts. They may even send you phony positive press releases that they created.

My advice: If a cold-calling salesperson or stranger begs you to buy a penny stock, don't listen. (In fact, never buy anything from someone who "cold-calls.") You may hear a pitch similar to this: "My dear friend, how would you like to buy a stock that is only 10 cents per share? For $1,000, you can own 10,000 shares. If the stock goes to a dollar, you could make $9,000. How does that sound? Can I count on you for a $1,000 investment? Trust me, this stock is hot."

One of the best movies on how easy it is to get lured into buying penny stocks and other undesirable investment products is the movie *Boiler Room* (2000). It shows what goes on behind the scenes in a "boiler room," where high-pressure salespeople are trained to convince unsuspecting investors to buy the junky penny stocks being sold.

Sadly, thousands of people fall for these investment scams every day, whether by email, phone, or the internet. The penny stockbrokers are skilled at making you feel that you are going to miss out on the deal of the decade if you don't buy in the next 10 minutes.

In reality, it's unlikely that the stock will ever claw its way out of the cellar. And if the stock is really that great, shouldn't the salespeople buy it themselves? Why are they calling strangers like you? The answer: They receive substantial commissions for every victim who buys the trash they are selling.

PUMP AND DUMP

Another popular but unethical scheme is when insiders at a small over-the-counter company make public pleas to potential victims to buy shares in their company because it's a "once in a lifetime" opportunity.

The fraudsters pump up interest in the stock by posting positive messages in chat rooms, sending mass emails, going on television or radio, and posting overly optimistic press releases and newsletters. Their goal is to artificially pump up the price of a stock, not because of solid fundamentals, but because of hype.

As the stock price goes higher (the pump), those who pumped the price prepare to sell at all-time highs (the dump). As more investors buy shares, insiders sell their positions at an artificially high price. Eventually, the stock price tanks.

Guess who is left holding the shares of the nearly worthless stock? You guessed it—the unsuspecting investors who believed the hype. They bought into the idea that the stock price could go even higher, so they never sold their shares.

The "pump and dump" is one of the oldest and most effective stock market schemes. Usually, pump and dumps are used on penny stocks selling for less than $3 per share because these stocks are so easy to manipulate.

The job of scammers is to earn your trust so they can separate you from your money. Once again, do not give money to strangers who call, text, or email.

NOTE: The opposite of pump and dump is "short and distort," when unethical short sellers say negative things about a company to try to push down its shares.

My opinion: Even with all the potential risks, if you are determined to trade (or "gamble with") the pennies, start small. With the skills you have already learned in this book, I hope that one day you shift out of the penny stock world and use your time to trade stocks in the major market indexes.

LEVERAGED ETFS: NOT RECOMMENDED

You already know that ETFs are an excellent idea. They provide instant diversification and trade just like stocks. However, there is one type of ETF, the *leveraged ETF*, that is extremely high risk.

Instead of the one-to-one return you receive with standard ETFs, leveraged ETFs can be two-to-one or three-to-one, that is, two or three times the return of the underlying index. The main purpose of a leveraged ETF is to amplify the returns of the underlying benchmark.

Here's the risk: Because of the complex way these leveraged products are constructed (using *derivatives* such as futures contracts, options, forward contracts, swaps, etc.), and because of tracking errors (i.e., when an ETF deviates from its benchmark), this product is undesirable for nearly everyone.

The only acceptable holding period for these puppies is one day, and not one day longer. In fact, the longer one holds one of these products, the poorer the performance.

Here is an example: With a "traditional" investment, if your asset rises by $5 one day and declines by $5 the next day, you are exactly even with neither gains nor losses. With a leveraged product, however, the asset actually loses value in that scenario. Let me explain.

Because the ETF portfolio must be constantly rebalanced, the added expenses paid for rebalancing increase over the long run. The bottom line is that the longer an investor holds leveraged ETFs, the less the return. Add in the higher fees and expenses and your potential gains are even worse than expected.

For this reason alone, leveraged ETFs, either long or short, are not recommended for anyone but the most experienced day traders. For them, trading leveraged ETFs might be desirable. But for everyone else, I suggest avoiding this product. There are plenty of non-leveraged ETFs that will meet your needs without venturing to the wild side.

The bottom line: Trade traditional, unleveraged ETFs, and you never have to be concerned about these matters. If you ignore my warnings and buy a leveraged ETF, do not hold it overnight.

HINT: If an ETF is described as being "ultra," it is a leveraged ETF.

. . . .

Now that you have a taste of high-risk, high-reward securities, let's see what happens when your worst financial nightmares come true: corrections, crashes, and bear markets.

In Part Five, you will learn not only how to prepare before one of these events occurs, but what to do about it when they do occur. Although it's not pleasant to think about a falling market, it's helpful to know what to expect. And if you like scary stories, you'll find it a very entertaining read.

CORRECTIONS, CRASHES, AND BEAR MARKETS

My original title for this section was "Open in Case of Emergency." When you experience any of the above events, you'll be glad these chapters are waiting for you. I discuss what to expect during a bear market, and include an interview with a bear market veteran who gives insights into how to survive when (not if) one arrives.

Truthfully, many long-only investors prefer not to think much about bear markets or crashes until they're in one. Others might be curious about what to expect (perhaps that's why you're reading this). I did my best to make it another entertaining and educational read.

When the market indexes fall by more than 20 percent, it results in a lower net worth for most people who invest. In a few short weeks, years of gains can be wiped out, causing severe emotional distress. The worst bear markets last for years.

A prolonged bear market is especially painful for those who work on Wall Street or for anyone invested in the stock market. Unless you are prepared in advance, it can be a life-changing experience, and not in a good way. One of the reasons you are reading this is to help you prepare for the inevitable.

Selling short is the first strategy discussed in Part Five. Selling short, a method for experienced traders, allows you to profit even when a stock or the market is moving lower. Although it may seem confusing to some novice investors, it's an important strategy to learn, especially during corrections, crashes, and bear markets.

CHAPTER 15

SELLING SHORT

I n this chapter, I discuss a fascinating but somewhat risky strategy: *selling short* (or *short selling*). When using this strategy, you profit when a stock or the overall market goes down. Some people believe it is unethical or unpatriotic to profit from a falling stock. I believe there is nothing unethical about it. After all, you're in the market for only one reason: to make money.

Short sellers are important for a free and independent stock market. The best professional short sellers poke holes in the "too good to be true" proclamations of the market bulls. They are able to expose potential financial problems in a company, and for that reason alone, short sellers serve an important role (even if bullish investors wish they would disappear).

Shorting stocks is a strategy best suited for experienced traders. The reason is simple: When you sell a stock that you don't own, you must buy back the stock eventually, and hopefully at a *lower* price. The risk is that if the stock moves *higher*, not lower, you lose money.

Shorting is a sophisticated strategy that earns profits during dismal economic conditions or when a specific stock runs into trouble. It's useful to learn the mechanics of this strategy, the reasons for using it, and the different ways you can profit from a falling stock or index. It's a worthwhile strategy so long as you are disciplined and use stop losses.

NOTE: Instead of shorting stocks, another choice is to buy inverse ETFs, explained later in this chapter.

THE BASICS OF SHORTING STOCKS

As you already know, when you invest in a stock hoping that its price will rise, you are said to be *long* the stock. Your goal is to buy at one price and eventually sell at a higher price. The profit is the difference between the buy price and the sale price multiplied by the number of shares.

On the other hand, when you are *short* a stock, you profit when the price of the stock you sold short falls. When shorting a stock, you first borrow shares of the stock from the brokerage, then sell the stock (shares that you don't own).

The goal is to buy the stock back (cover the short) at a lower price. If you have never shorted stocks, it may sound strange until you do it a few times. It shouldn't matter whether you are long or short, as long as you make profits.

A SHORT EXAMPLE: HOW IT'S DONE

Let's say you are watching a stock, YYYY, and believe that its price will move lower over the next month. Perhaps there is negative news about the company or you notice that the firm has recently taken on a lot of debt that could impact its cash flow. You decide to short 100 shares of YYYY at the current price of $40 per share.

To execute this trade, on your brokerage screen, select a limit order to "Sell YYYY" or "Sell Short." Because you don't own the stock, the brokerage software will automatically "lend" you 100 shares of YYYY at $40 per share.

The $4,000 ($40 × 100) sale price is deposited into your margin account. Here's the interesting part: If YYYY falls to $38 per share, you can lock in the $200 profit by buying back the 100 shares (select "Buy to Close" on your brokerage screen).

After pressing the Enter key, you earned a $200 profit. The borrowed shares are returned to the lender, and you can move to the next trade.

WHAT CAN GO WRONG

Although selling short is a straightforward strategy, a lot of things can go wrong. First, when you buy stock, the most you can lose is the amount that you invested. That's pretty painful, but how much can you lose when shorting? The answer is frightening: an infinite amount. When a stock is sold short, there is no theoretical limit on how high the price can rise.

For example, let's say there's an earnings release on YYYY. Instead of moving lower as you expected, YYYY rallies. Because you were wrong, for every point YYYY increases, you lose $100. Therefore, if YYYY continues to move higher and higher, your losses continue to pile up.

This is the main reason why shorting has a bad reputation. If you are not disciplined and allow losses to continue with little or no risk management, you could lose a lot of money.

Nevertheless, most experienced short sellers are disciplined enough to cover (close their short positions) when the stock price moves against them. Also, if a client loses too much money on a short position, the brokerage will call—this is the dreaded *margin call*. The short seller must deposit additional funds into the account, or the position will be closed.

This is not the kind of strategy that you initiate and then go on vacation. If you short an individual stock, it must be watched closely until the position is covered. (You can also use a *buy stop order*—an automatic order to buy back the stock when it reaches a specific price).

> **NOTE:** If you do short, it's essential to limit potential losses to no more than 10 percent with a stop-loss order. It's also recommended that you short with a small position, especially if you have never used this strategy before.
>
> I also recommend making dozens of practice short trades before using real money. Potential losses can accumulate rather quickly, which is why this strategy should only be used on occasion, and always with extreme caution.

To eliminate the risks associated with short selling (that is, unlimited losses), there is an alternative method for making money when the indexes fall. This method, buying *inverse ETFs*, is explained later in this chapter. Although there are risks associated with buying inverse ETFs, at least your potential losses aren't unlimited.

Now that you know the shorting basics, let's explore how to use this strategy.

HOW TO FIND WINNING SHORT CANDIDATES

The good news about shorting is that it's not difficult to find stocks that are weak and trending lower. If you are shorting, you must think in reverse from how long-term investors think. Look for stocks in a downtrend, and then follow them lower. Here are some ideas:

- Find stocks that are at or near their 52-week lows. This list can be found on MarketWatch, CNN Money, Yahoo Finance, Google Finance, and Market Chameleon, to name a few. While some traders may short these stocks, buy-the-dippers may go long. These are two opposing strategies but only one makes it to the winner's circle.

- Find stocks that are trending lower in the premarket. The most active stocks that are about to decline right out of the starting gate can be found on the websites mentioned above (and many others).

- Run a scan on your broker's trading software. Most brokers offer the ability to scan for premarket losers, or whichever financial criteria you enter.

- Be attentive to stocks that are mentioned in the news before the market opens. Be careful, because some of the stocks with negative headlines may sink at the open and reverse direction within minutes.

     This is one of the risks of shorting. If buy-the-dip algos decide to initiate a bull raid on a stock you're shorting, the financial pain you'll feel could be indescribable (see the sidebar "The Short Squeeze" for a worst-case scenario).

- Short the weakest stocks in the weakest sectors. Avoid stocks that already have a heavy *short interest*. Believe it or not, some of the strongest stocks in the world are often the most shorted: Apple, Amazon, and Microsoft, to name a few.

NOTE: *Short interest* is the number of shares of a given stock that have been sold short. Expressed as a percentage, short interest is the fraction of the total number of outstanding shares that investors are currently holding as a short position. Many traders use it as an indicator of market sentiment. For example, high short interest shows that investors are pessimistic about that stock.

To find stocks with short interest, visit financial sites including Finviz.com. Most stocks that have high short interest have at least 20 percent of the total share float sold short (this is a rough estimate).

Before selling short, be on the lookout for the technical signals presented in the following sidebar.

TECHNICAL SHORT SIGNALS

- **Moving averages.** Look for stocks that broke *below* their 20-, 50-, or 100-day moving averages (or use shorter periods if you are an intraday short seller).

- **MACD.** If shorting, MACD must be on your side (MACD must be below the zero line and below the signal line). In addition, look for bearish divergences, as they give meaningful signals (although the signal is slower than that from stochastics). You can also use MACD to identify whether your stock or ETF is at risk of reversing.

- **MACD histogram.** As a short seller, you want to see price momentum decrease on the way up and increase on the way down.

- **Slow Stochastic.** You want to see %K and %D moving lower. However, if %K and %D are at 20 or below (oversold), and the signals cross, that is a confirmed buy signal. Short sellers must be extremely careful when stocks get oversold because reversals are very common.

- **RSI.** Use RSI to identify whether your stock or ETF is *oversold*. However, if you notice that RSI suddenly turns higher, it's possible the stock price is building upside momentum. It's not necessarily a "get out now" signal if short, but you'd better be on guard.

  Again, don't hold an oversold stock for too long. You don't want to get trapped in a short position when the algos decide to conduct a bull raid.

- **Volatility.** Inexperienced short sellers often take a short position as a stock moves higher. Their biggest mistake is failing to look at oscillators such as Bollinger Bands or RSI. If the sellers had noticed that volatility was expanding while a stock (even an overbought one) moved higher, they would have known that it was simply too risky to short at that time.

A wiser approach is to wait for volatility to peak and then *contract*. This is your clue to probe on the short side. Note that I wrote "probe." If you are shorting, don't make the common mistake of making a huge one-time lump-sum bet. If wrong, you will feel like you've been caught swimming naked when the tide goes out (to paraphrase Warren Buffett).

• **Support and resistance.** You are on the right side if the stock price breaks below support levels, and technical indicators turn negative. As a short seller, ride the downtrend as long as you can, but be very cautious (for reasons mentioned above). Individual short sellers each have their own selling criteria using the technical indicators in this book.

• **Candlesticks.** If candlesticks turn from green to red and other bearish candlestick patterns appear, pay attention. Maybe something bad is happening to the stock (which is good for you when short).

NOTE: If using fundamental analysis, search for stocks with negative information such as missed earnings, poor management decisions, lackluster sales, or accounting irregularities. Any of these problems affects the stock price, and not in a good way.

. . . .

SHORT WHAT YOU KNOW

Peter Lynch famously said that you should "invest in what you know." He suggested that investors visit the mall or stores to get stock ideas. With those ideas, he said to do additional research until you find a company that has strong earnings and little debt.

As a short seller, you can also use Lynch's methods but in reverse. For example, if you were at the mall several years ago, you may have noticed that while everyone was shopping at Apple, there were few customers at Sears. Guess what happened? The stock price of Apple kept going higher, while Sears's stock sank lower until the company eventually went bankrupt.

Although Sears was one of the most popular companies in the world at one time, upper management was slow to move its products to the internet. Eventually, people did their shopping online—and the rest is history.

The point is that if you are a short seller, look for companies with weak earnings, little foot traffic, and a lot of debt. Those are the types of companies you may consider shorting.

By the way, anyone who shorted Sears would have made good profits, as shares of Sears fell from their all-time high of $195 in 2007 to penny stock status 10 years later. It's not the fault of the short sellers that Sears fell from grace. Blame the CEO and upper management for running a once great company into the ground.

IT "HAS" TO GO DOWN

I know a lot of short sellers who target a certain stock (Tesla was a favorite) because it just "has to go down." Guess what? If you short a stock because of some rule that you made up, such as a stock can't go higher by more than "x number" of days, your days as a successful short seller will be *short* (pun intended).

After all, no one ever knows how high the market or stocks can rise. Even stocks that are obscenely overbought can keep going higher (and they often do). Wall Street is littered with the graves of short sellers whose last words were, "It can't keep going up forever!"

THE TRUTH: It may not go up forever, but it could go up for long enough to wipe out your trading account. Anything is possible in the stock market.

TIPS AND TRICKS

For anyone who is serious about using this strategy, here are a few tips and tricks:

- Before shorting, call your broker to make sure that you can borrow the shares. Some brokers post on their trading platform whether a stock is available for shorting. They may have codes such as ETB (easy to borrow) or HTB (hard to borrow). With some small-cap stocks, it may be difficult to find shares to short. Also, ask the broker if there are any fees to short these stocks.
- Adding insult to injury, when shorting, you are obligated to pay the dividend on the ex-dividend date. It may be a small amount, but some stocks have large dividends, which must be paid. An example: The dividend is $1.00 and you are short 200 shares. It's not a deal breaker, but in this example, you owe $200 on the ex-dividend date.

    HINT: Run a scan or check the Stock Statistics page to find out the ex-dividend date and the amount of the dividend. An excellent source is MarketWatch (look for the dividend calendar), but your broker should also have this information.

- Never short a stock in front of an earnings release. Earnings are usually reported when the markets are closed. If you're on the wrong side of this event (that is, the earnings exceed expectations), you might wake up to extremely painful losses.

> **HINT:** If you are short selling, never get caught unprepared or trapped by unexpected events such as an earnings release, a Fed meeting, or negative news. Knowledge is your ally.

- Consider covering short positions on deep down days, as snapback rallies are common the next day. This is not a rule, as some stocks keep falling, but always be on guard for reversals.

THE BIG SHORT

If you want a real-life example of the agony that professional short sellers experienced, you can watch the excellent movie *The Big Short* (or read the book by Michael Lewis). The biographical drama explores the experiences of hedge fund manager Michael Burry and other short sellers.

After a thorough analysis, Burry concluded that the 2008 real estate market was in a bubble and would collapse—especially *subprime mortgages*. Burry shorted the housing market using complicated derivative contracts (*credit default swaps*).

Here's the infuriating part: Even though Burry was right, he was early. Remember when I spoke about unlimited losses when shorting? Burry and other short sellers suffered through immeasurable pain as their positions continued to lose money when the underlying securities went higher and higher. During this time, Burry and other short sellers sustained millions of dollars in losses.

The average Jane or Joe would not have been able to hold losing positions for that long. These pros were certain they were right, based on extensive research, and had the capital to withstand the financial damage, but the housing market bubble kept expanding—until one day, it popped.

That was the day that Lehman Brothers collapsed, filing for bankruptcy along with Bear Stearns. That was also when Burry and other short sellers made hundreds of millions of dollars on their short positions.

THE LESSON: Even when short sellers are right, they often lose money if they are too early.

SHORTING STOCKS WITH INVERSE ETFS

If you are intimidated by the idea of selling stocks short, there is an easier way: Buy *inverse* ETFs (exchange-traded funds). The fund manager attempts to mimic the performance of a theoretical basket of stocks that have been sold short. Here's the important part: When the individual stocks in the ETF move *lower*, the price of the ETF moves *higher*.

Here's why inverse ETFs are useful: Let's say that you believe the S&P 500 is going to drop over the next month. Instead of shorting specific stocks, which would require a large margin account, you can buy an inverse ETF.

To come to this conclusion, you must have valid fundamental or technical reasons, not just a hunch. Receiving a tip from a friend or reading a scary article warning of an imminent crash is not a valid reason to make this trade.

The advantage of buying an inverse ETF is its simplicity. Unlike selling short individual stocks, you let the ETF do the shorting for you. Even more interesting, inverse ETFs are available for the major indexes such as the S&P 500 and Nasdaq and for hundreds of other indexes and stock sectors.

Here's a specific example of how they work: If the S&P 500 moves lower by 1 percent today, then the inverse ETF will move *higher* by approximately 1 percent. Conversely, if the S&P 500 moves *higher* by 1 percent, then the inverse ETF will move *lower* by approximately 1 percent. The inverse ETF is designed to move on a one-to-one percentage with the S&P 500, but in reverse.

As you can see, it's a lot easier to buy an inverse ETF than to short individual stocks. In addition, the most you can lose if the trade is wrong is your entire investment, but no more. As you already know, with traditional shorting strategies, you could lose more than you invested. Hence, buying inverse ETFs might be a desirable strategy for anyone wanting to bet the market is going to fall.

> **NOTE:** An example of an inverse ETF is the ProShares Short S&P 500 (symbol: SH) or the ProShares Short QQQ ETF (symbol: PSQ).

> **NOTE:** Not everyone is a fan of inverse ETFs because they sometimes contain financial instruments too complicated to explain here (for example, *derivatives* and *swaps*). That is why some critics believe inverse ETFs are better suited to day traders; nevertheless, these products are *not* designed for a long-term buy and hold.

> **WARNING:** You already know from reading Chapter 14 that you should not buy *leveraged* ETFs, and that includes not buying *leveraged inverse ETFs*. Leveraged products are only for day traders and substantially increase the risks primarily because of the way they are constructed (for example, through tracking errors).

THE SHORT SQUEEZE

If a stock suddenly moves up to astonishingly high levels in a short time period, it may be due to a painful phenomenon called a *short squeeze*. Get on the wrong side of one of these events, and all you can do is watch your account get decimated. A short squeeze puts fear and panic in the hearts of all short sellers.

Short sellers are always one Fed announcement or one positive earnings report away from a disastrous loss. This happens routinely to many hapless rookies, but rarely do the pros get burned.

That is, until January 2021, when the poster child for short squeezes occurred with GameStop, a struggling brick-and-mortar retailer. It turned out to be a momentum trader's dream and a short seller's nightmare.

GameStop was not a favorite by many on Wall Street, one of the reasons many pros held short positions. Unbeknown to the pros who worked for several hedge funds, thousands of retail investors gathered on Reddit, a popular internet forum, to simultaneously buy GameStop (GME). It was a coordinated "bull raid" but became more like a buying frenzy.

After traders on Reddit collectively bought millions of shares, GME surged by over 1,500 percent within two weeks, sending volatility and the stock price "to the moon," from less than $3 per share to $483 in less than two months.

Anyone who was short this video game retailer got smashed. Melvin Capital, an investment fund that heavily shorted GameStop, reportedly lost hundreds of millions on the trade. It was also reported that some hedge funds, along with thousands of retail short sellers, collectively lost $6 billion (and their shirts) on this one trade.

Trading on GameStop (and AMC, another "meme" stock that was short squeezed) was halted as the hedge funds counted their losses. This was one of those rare times when the little guy beat Wall Street, leaving Wall Street shocked for weeks.

The traders who lost the most money in GameStop and AMC were those who sold "naked" calls (that is, they sold options on stocks they didn't own).

It wasn't just the short sellers who got hurt. Brokers shared headshaking stories about clients who cleared out their retirement funds or took cash advances on their credit cards so they could buy GameStop and AMC after the short squeeze was over. Some won, some lost, but many investors learned that they had taken on way too much risk.

· · · · · · · · ·

Now that you have learned how to short stocks as well as buy inverse ETFs, you will be in a better position to thrive when the market plunges. Speaking of plunging, if you're willing to read more financial horror stories, you've come to the right place. In Chapter 16, you will enter a trading environment where the mind is more powerful than matter.

CHAPTER 16

BEAR MARKET STRATEGIES

I f you are reading this during a correction, crash, or bear market, you are at the right place. Perhaps you're reading this so you'll be prepared in case something bad happens to the market. Whatever the reason, I believe this chapter will be an educational and eye-opening read.

Truthfully, few market participants want to think about market pullbacks or corrections, and who can blame them? Those conditions are not pleasant for most people. Fortunately, there are ways to not only survive a major downturn, but to thrive. By the time you finish Part Five, you will learn a number of strategies and tactics that may help.

NOTE: If you're reading this chapter during a bull market, you may think this is much ado about nothing. Perhaps you believe the Fed has figured out a way to make bear markets a thing of the past. I assure you that's not possible.

After all, as long as there is a stock market, there will be corrections, crashes, and bear markets. The challenge is predicting when one of these events will occur, and the truth is that no one can predict their arrival, though many people continue to try.

NOTE: In previous chapters, I've offered ideas about how to use technical indicators to identify when a bullish trend is ending.

My hope is that you can use some of those same tools to help protect your account in case Wall Street is visited by a big, bad bear.

Let's begin our discussion with definitions.

DEFINITIONS, PLEASE

The official definition of a *bear market* is a drop of 20 percent or more from the previous high. A *crash*, on the other hand, is a sudden, violent plunge in the market by at least 20 percent. If it's "only" a 10 percent pullback, it's considered to be a *correction*.

Typically, corrections and crashes don't persist for a long time, while bear markets can last as little as a month or two or as long as a year (and sometimes longer).

I don't want to leave you with the impression that a market correction or crash is not a big deal, because it is, especially for those who feel like sitting ducks when their portfolios slide by 20, 30, or 50 percent.

It's terrible for these investors and their families. In a worst-case scenario, it could take years for the market to recover, and some stocks never do.

The only good news is that corrections or crashes don't usually last long, because fear and panic often subside quickly. It is at this point when bargain hunters enter the market. A correction is like a pinprick when compared with a crash. As you'll discover later in this chapter, a bear market is an entirely different animal.

What Is a Correction?

As noted above, to qualify as a correction, the market indexes must drop by at least 10 percent from the recent highs. Corrections can last from a few weeks to several months. Technicians consider corrections to be healthy because they help to bring overbought markets back to reality. Every once in a while, overly exuberant investors are reminded that markets do fall.

Even corrections can be painful for anyone who hasn't taken steps to limit risk. Risk management includes diversifying into different investments or sectors, not using margin or leveraged products, and having cash on the side when possible.

What Is a Crash?

A crash is a sudden, violent, short-lived plunge in the stock market. The word *crash* has struck fear in the hearts and minds of investors and traders since the stock market was created. Since then, there have been dozens of crashes, with the worst occurring in 1929. Although we hope a crash of that magnitude never repeats, anything is possible. The only good news about crashes is they are usually short-lived events.

During a crash, market indexes drop quickly and unexpectedly, and by more than 20 percent. Crashes appear out of nowhere, although in hindsight there were plenty of clues and warning signs.

Most investors are caught off guard and shocked at the financial damage. When markets are rising and investors are smiling, few believe that the market could go that low. It's not uncommon to see entire portfolios wiped out in a few days or weeks. Some investors never recover.

As long as they haven't taken extreme risks, most market participants survive, though with considerably less money in their investment accounts. You need a strong stomach to not do anything rash, such as selling in a panic during a crash. Many investors make irrational decisions during these times as the market keeps plunging.

HINT: A well-thought-out plan including stop-loss orders can eliminate a large portion of losses in a crash.

THE DAY OF THE CRASH

I have met several individuals who were wiped out during a crash. It has the potential to ruin lives and livelihoods. Emotions run high and fear is rampant during the event.

On the day of the crash, because panicked traders and investors enter a slew of sell orders electronically, brokerage firms probably won't answer their phones until after the market closes. Brokerage websites have been known to shut down during extreme downside moves (the flash crash on May 6, 2010, is a good example). That means you probably won't be able to trade online on that day; all you can do is wait until there is a temporary lull in the mass selling.

When everyone is trying to sell at once, the crash intensifies, causing other investors and traders to panic. Typically, when there's a crash in one country's market, it spreads to other countries around the world, and may result in a worldwide sell-off.

It doesn't help when breaking news on the internet and nearly every newspaper is yelling, "Crash!" If you are caught holding the bag during this time, it's wise to avoid making any important financial decisions. This isn't the time to follow the panicked herd and sell.

When the panic eventually subsides—and after a few days it usually does—the Fed may work feverishly behind the scenes to lower interest rates and use a variety of tools to stabilize the market. If the efforts of the Fed are successful, the crash will be short-lived.

SEARCHING FOR BARGAINS AMID THE RUINS

Markets typically bounce back after a major crash. Astute traders monitor the markets closely for a *dead cat bounce*, another term for a failed rally. Sometimes the rally doesn't fail and the market really does bounce back, which is good news for investors.

Instead of hiding, it may be a good time to search for potential buying opportunities. If the crash is short-lived, which is nearly everyone's hope, buying the dip may prove to be an ideal strategy.

In the past, some of the world's greatest companies went on sale during a crash. After a crash, stocks that were selling for $400 per share may be selling for $300 or less. It's not easy to buy when everyone else is selling. If you have any cash on the side, this may be the time to scale into the market.

Admittedly, it is not an easy trading environment. The first major rally after the crash could be only temporary, what is called a *bear market rally*. These fake rallies suck in many bullish investors before the market sinks again.

HINT: After a correction or crash, watch the rallies. If the market continues moving higher, with stocks rising above their moving averages on strong volume, that is a bullish signal, and perhaps the worst may be over. If the technical indicators confirm that the rally has legs, take this as a good time to scale into the market.

I don't want you to think that it's easy to buy the dip after a crash. The market will be incredibly volatile during this period, with 3 to 5 percent moves in either direction occurring frequently. Emotions are running high, and it's easy to make dumb mistakes or succumb to your fears. For many, the smartest move is to do nothing. If you step into the market during these wild times, it's easy to get fooled.

WHAT IS A BEAR MARKET?

Bear markets are a different animal from a crash. Some are short-lived, lasting only a few months, while others typically last a year or longer. The 2002 bear market was officially one of the longest at 929 days, ruining the lives and financial dreams of many.

Lengthy bear markets are terrible for those who work on Wall Street or for anyone who owns stock. Although the odds are good that you will experience a bear market one day, I hope for your sake that it is short-lived.

> **NOTE:** While a correction or crash isn't enjoyable, it is survivable because it doesn't last very long. On the other hand, it's hard for people to make it through a lengthy bear market without emotional and financial scars.

THE DAY OF RECKONING: HOW TO PREPARE

During a bear market, there is almost always a day of reckoning. That's when it seems as if everyone collectively heads for the exits at the same time. On that day, those who ignored risk or volatility may suddenly discover that they can no longer tolerate the pain and bail out of positions. Often, that becomes the market low.

The reason you are reading this chapter is to avoid getting trapped. Well before a crash or bear market arrives, the key is always thinking of ways to reduce risk. If you can do that, then you can survive whatever the market throws at you.

While a crash cannot be predicted, you can take steps to limit the damage. The last thing you want to do is run around like Chicken Little. However, the time to prepare is *before* a correction or crash occurs.

Just like preparing for a hurricane, the first step is to create a written disaster plan of what to do. Periodically review your holdings and the sum allocated to each investment. While you don't want to react to every 5 percent drop in the market, don't be complacent.

In fact, when years or even a decade goes by when the market has only moved higher, some investors will begin to believe the market "will never go down again." That unrealistic belief probably means they will be unprepared for the next downturn. In many ways, complacency is nearly as dangerous as fear.

> **NOTE:** I'm not trying to frighten you, but only provide you with the facts so you know what to expect before a bear market arrives. While a crash comes and goes quickly, prolonged bear markets are the most destructive. They can last longer than many investors believe.

The following sidebar describes some of the signals to look for when a bear market arrives.

CORRECTION, CRASH, OR BEAR MARKET SIGNALS

- **Moving averages.** Stocks break below their 50- and 100-day moving averages, sometimes very quickly. During a bear market, stocks will remain below their moving averages for a long time period.
- **MACD.** The MACD line moves below the zero line and 9-day signal line. Although it's a lagging indicator, look for signs of a reversal. When MACD rises back above the zero line and the 9-day signal line, it may be the time to go long again.
- **MACD histogram.** The MACD histogram bars darken as the markets fall. Use the histogram to help determine when the worst is over. Look for the histogram to lighten as momentum strengthens. That is a clue that prices may follow to the upside.
- **Slow Stochastic.** %K and %D will fall until severely oversold (below 20). If %K and %D drop below 20 and cross, that is a buy signal. Stochastics may give false signals, so trade cautiously during volatile market conditions.

- **RSI.** During and after a crash or bear market, RSI drops below 30, a severely oversold reading. Look for RSI to turn back above 30, which may be a clue to go long again. If you are a short-term trader, prepare to abandon long positions in case the rally fails.

- **Volatility.** Volatility explodes during and after a crash and increases during a bear market. Experienced short-term traders have the potential to profit during these times, but it isn't easy. Many traders buy the dip and short the rallies, but only the best survive.

  The VIX will zoom to 50 and above during a correction or crash, but typically that won't last long. These are wild times, so it's easy to make or lose money. Beginners should trade small or not at all during these volatile events.

- **Support and resistance.** The major indexes will plummet below support levels and stay below. When the market eventually recovers, indexes will rise above resistance and stay above. If that happens, the rally could have legs, a signal that it's time to go long again.

· · · · · · · ·

THE PSYCHOLOGY OF A BEAR MARKET

Because I grew up in a family of stockbrokers, I witnessed the power of a vicious, long-lasting bear market. In our house, a bear market was treated like a swear word. The first clue of trouble was when my father asked us to turn off the lights to save on electricity.

I don't mean that you should go through life being afraid of a bear market. My advice to you: Don't succumb to your emotions. You're reading this chapter because you want to be mentally prepared for a worst-case scenario.

When a bear market begins, few admit that the bear has come out of hibernation. Just like in my house, no one on Wall Street mentions the term. It's also not a popular topic at a party or barbeque.

During the lowest points of a bear market, many come to believe that the market will never go up again, just like they thought it would always go higher. However, and this is important, the market *will* stop going down and the bear market *will* end; it's just that no one knows when.

FIGHT OR FLEE

The causes of a bear market are not as important as recognizing one when it appears. Some investors bury their heads in the sand, refuse to look at their brokerage statements, and say to their broker, "Wake me up when it's over."

To survive a bear market, it is essential to keep a clear head. This is not the time to panic or listen to touts who warn of even worse conditions. Weeks or months before, these same individuals were giddy and overconfident, bragging on Twitter about their lavish lifestyles, acting as if the market would never go down. Now, you see them on TV with shaky voices.

SHOULD YOU SELL DURING A BEAR MARKET?

While nearly every investor claims to buy low and sell high, when indexes are plunging and fear is rampant, people discard that strategy and try to exit before their paper losses get worse.

Don't get me wrong: I am not advising you to avoid selling during a bear market. I am saying to be strategic and unemotional about it. Sell if you have valid technical or fundamental reasons based on logic, clues, and indicators.

Just don't sell in a panic because you "think" the market is going to keep going lower. Even worse, don't listen to acquaintances who are also panicked and urge you to follow them into the abyss.

WATCH THE RALLIES

Bear market expert Mark D. Cook often said that the key to understanding a bear market is to watch the rallies. Sometimes there are strong rallies in the middle of a bear market, something that he'd call "one-day wonders." Other times, the rallies were anemic, which was a clue the bear market might linger.

WHAT TO DO DURING A BEAR MARKET

Because every bear market is different, I can only offer guidelines, not specific rules. If the bear market is a short-lived affair, then it will come and go so quickly that most investors won't feel the effects.

If it's a long-lasting bear market nightmare, it may take more time and cause more damage than most investors are prepared for. The hope is that you are diversified and your portfolio includes alternative investments such as gold, bonds, and perhaps even digital currencies. The idea is to spread the risk instead of being concentrated into only stocks.

Cash is usually king during a bear market, despite low interest rates. Another choice is to buy bonds, which may provide a safe haven during a bear market, depending on interest rates. If the Fed lowers interest rates during a bear market, bonds or bond mutual funds may be an excellent choice.

THE BAD NEWS BEARS

During the deepest depths of a bear market, when the pain is the most excruciating, ignore the noise and continue to look at technical indicators. Many oscillators may show extreme oversold conditions, which serve as a clue that a reversal is possible.

When stocks or the market gets so extremely overbought, and valuations seem to be in the Twilight Zone, going long is like playing with fire. Be patient before buying the dip.

Many investors, scarred by the effects of a destructive bear market, may swear off the stock market forever. Guess what? This is often the best time to shake off your fears and invest.

LOOMING SIGNS OF A BEAR MARKET

This sidebar is based on my conversations with the late trader Mark D. Cook, an expert on bear markets. In a lengthy interview, he told me the 10 stages of a bear market. Since every bear market is different, it's possible that these may occur in a different order than listed here.

1. Failed Rallies

One of the first clues of an impending bear market is the rallies. If the market does not rally strongly, or cannot hold its gains, this is a clue the market is wounded. It will be vulnerable to further injury if there are "lower lows" and "lower highs" on the chart.

2. Low-Volume Rallies

The rallies are tepid, weak, and lifeless in a low-volume environment. This is a clue the institutions are not buying. Typically, institutions are a herd, and they watch their peers closely. If the entire pack doesn't follow in lockstep immediately, the rally falters. You will hear people say, "This time is different, and history won't repeat itself." Here's some breaking news: History always repeats itself.

If the market is unable to bounce back quickly or with any zeal after a sell-off, and if it cannot retrace at least half of the bounce, that's a red flag. The bear market is near.

3. Ugly-Looking Charts

Another clue comes from the charts. A lower low on the chart tells technicians that the mood of the once invincible market is vulnerable. Technicians who study charts believe that if the market closes with lower lows, buyers will start leaving.

The stubborn bulls hold their positions, but sweat beads appear on their brows. They say to themselves, "I can't sell here." So they don't.

4. Strong Sell-offs

The market begins to accelerate to the downside by shedding scores of S&P 500 points every few days. On the up days, the S&P 500 is labored and slow, and rallies are small. The downward moves are much faster and deeper.

At this stage, bullish investors are still buying the dips, but not as enthusiastically. Therefore, the volume during declines is increasing, while the rallies are not as energetic. Nevertheless, most bulls aren't thinking of selling (a stage they don't reach until it's too late).

5. Mutual Fund Redemptions

The market has fallen into a correction. On a chart, the market makes a lower low for the entire quarter. Now that portfolios are down by 15 or 20 percent, bullish investors are thinking of selling. A 20 percent decline triggers mutual fund redemptions. Even some money managers are thinking of selling as the sell-off intensifies.

6. From Complacency to Panic

Institutions are lightening their positions because they fear investor withdrawals. The negative quarter irritates investors, the first clue that their mood is changing. Eventually, investors move from complacent peacefulness to terrified panic, but this takes time. The most stubborn bulls haven't liquidated their positions, but they're buying less. In due time, the market will give up all its previous gains.

7. All News Is Bad News

As the bear market picks up speed, there is less good news. Economic releases are now viewed with more skepticism. Analysts focus on the bad news while suspicious of any good economic news. Some stubborn bulls are still holding, but their sweat beads have become torrents.

8. Institutions Are Forced to Sell

Some bulls can't take it anymore. As the volume increases with consecutive down days, stubborn bulls have finally thrown in the towel. After they have lost over 20 percent, many hope the worst is over. These people believe the Fed will save them just as it did in the past.

As the market keeps falling, many institutions are forced to get out because of investor redemptions. At this point, the Fed is ignored, and it's a free-for-all. Numerous investors are lost and confused.

9. A Bear Market Is Declared

Since the market is down by 20 percent or more and hasn't bounced, the media proclaim a bear market. It's even possible the market is down by as much as 30 percent. Brokers are telling nervous clients not to sell.

As the bear market receives front-page attention on all the networks and the internet, many bulls liquidate their positions. Red ink has replaced what were gains only months earlier. Volatility increases each day, as huge down days are more prevalent.

10. Capitulation

After weeks or months of sell-offs, many investors look at their statements and panic. When they realize their portfolios aren't coming back to even anytime soon, they capitulate. Volume will be greater than three times normal.

At this point, the market is overheating and may blow a gasket. Financial firms are near collapse, and more firms are in trouble. Bulls liquidate nearly all their positions, turning once profitable portfolios into a sea of blood. Many brokerage statements reveal equity losses of 40 or 50 percent and sometimes more.

Investors lose confidence in the market as brokerage firms liquidate the portfolios of traders who used margin. The market is hated, and some investors vow never to return. Years of market gains are in tatters. No asset class is considered safe, as all financial products fall together.

· · · · · · · ·

I hope that you never experience the financial horror story you just read, but at least now you know what is possible. I'm going to continue our bear market discussion by telling you how the pros handle bear markets. One is a professional short seller, and two are long-term investors. As you will see, each handles bear markets in a different way.

CHAPTER 17

HOW PROS MANAGE BEAR MARKETS

n this chapter, I tell you how three pros manage bear markets. One is a trader, and two are investors, and each has his own method that has worked for him. As you will soon see, the advice ranges from doing nothing to trying to profit from the extreme volatility.

I'll begin with two successful investors and how they manage bear markets. If you're an investor, their advice should bring you some comfort, as they both advise you to stay the course.

In other words, if it appears that a bear market won't end anytime soon, read the calming words of these veterans and know that one day the Bad News Bears will go away, often when it appears there is no hope.

PETER LYNCH

In my previous book, *Understanding Stocks*, I shared a lengthy discussion with Peter Lynch, whom many consider as the greatest fund manager in history. In the 1990s he had a spectacular 29.2 percent average yearly return over 13 years, beating 99 percent of all equity funds at that time. He is also the author of three bestselling books, including *One Up on Wall Street* (Simon & Schuster).

I had the opportunity to ask him about his handling of bear markets, and his advice was simple and amusing: "If you understand what companies you own and who their competitors are, you're in good shape. You don't panic if the market declines and the stock goes down. If you don't understand what a company does and the stock price falls by half, what should you do? If you haven't done your research, you might as well call a psychic hotline for investment advice."

Lynch adds that if you plan to sell your stock in a panic because the market falls by 10 or 20 percent, "you shouldn't be in the stock market in the first place. One of the great lines is, 'More money has been lost worrying about corrections than by the correction itself.'"

He says that "the most important organ in your body is not the brain; it's the stomach. If you let your stomach rule, you'll get shaken up, because when the market goes down, you will probably sell."

The key, he explains, is to ignore the negative background noise: "If the market goes down by 10 percent or more, the talk shows are negative, the news shows are negative, and there is a lot of pessimism. By 7:15 a.m. you're already in a bad mood."

What should an investor do when the market tumbles? He advises: "As long as you don't need the money in the next 10, 20, or 30 years for a wedding or your kid's college, I would be comfortable about being in the stock market. This is what makes a good investor."

Lynch says that sometimes the best time to buy or add to your position is when the market and the economy seem terrible. "That," he says, "is why the stomach is your most important organ."

JOHN BOGLE

I also had the opportunity to interview the late John Bogle several times over many years. He was the founder and former CEO of the Vanguard Group. He created the world's first index fund in 1976 and unsurprisingly was a huge proponent of indexing.

I knew that Bogle had experienced several bear markets in his lifetime, so I asked him what he would do if he saw another one coming. Would he still hold the index fund?

He immediately replied: "Yes. First, you should be properly diversified and your asset allocation must be right. Sixty percent stocks and forty percent bonds is a good place to start. If you see a bear market developing in advance, you must get out at the height of the market, and jump back when it hits its lows. But I don't know anyone who can tell you precisely when a bear market is going to begin, and I certainly can't tell you when it's going to end. That means you have to be right twice. The chances of that are so small that you should just stick to your long-term investment plan. It's great advice to tell me to get out of stocks before a bear market. But can you drop me a note when it's time to get back in? I think investors should stay the course whether it's a bear market or not. Don't try to outsmart the market."

I followed up with, "What do you suggest that investors do?"

He replied: "Don't pay too much attention to the daily gyrations of the stock market. If you have a diversified portfolio with low costs, simply stay the course. Yes, you would have been right if you got out at the high and back in at the low, but I not only don't know anybody who actually did so, I don't know anyone who knows anyone who did it."

· · · · · · · · ·

If you're reading this during a vicious bear market, I hope that the advice from these two successful market veterans helps calm your nerves. They both make it clear that you don't have to use complicated strategies to make money in the market.

When the inevitable bear market comes, there is no need to panic, as it will eventually pass. If you know what you own, as Lynch said, you will be in good shape when it's over.

MARK D. COOK

Mark D. Cook was an expert on crashes and bear markets. He experienced the destructive power of a crash when he worked for one of the top brokerage firms in the country, E.F. Hutton. The brokerage had a popular advertisement, "When E.F. Hutton talks, people listen."

As a reward, in July 1987 the company took 250 of its top brokers to Manhattan. The company had just finished construction of a beautiful new building that Cook said was the "most opulent thing you ever saw. A few of the brokers joked that this must be a market top. It turned out they were right."

"Think about this," Cook said. "In July, E.F. Hutton was one of the best in the industry. By October, there was no more E.F. Hutton! They went from King of the Hill to a name found in the history books."

Cook said that the actual market top occurred three months earlier than the October 1987 crash, but few knew it at the time. One clue was that the bond market started tanking three or four months earlier, and that led the stock market lower.

After the crash, the fallout was devastating. "We went from an all-time high to a massacre," Cook noted. The market gave back 18 months of gains in six weeks.

Needing a scapegoat, people blamed computerized trading for the crash.

No Fear

Instead of being afraid of bear markets, Cook learned to profit from them. Similar to hurricane hunters who fly into the eye of the storm, Cook looked forward to the next bear market. He was in awe of the destructive power of bear markets but also respected them.

Cook said that a monster crash is not good for anyone. He preferred to see a correction, where he makes the most money. He noted:

"I hope it's only a 10 or 20 percent correction. Then volatility will return to the market. On the other hand, after a major crash, there are few opportunities to trade at first, because volatility is anemic."

Cook, an old-fashioned "tape reader," relied primarily on his favorite indicator, the NYSE TICK (this indicator compares the number of rising stocks with the number of falling stocks on the NYSE).

Before Cook passed away, he was shocked that the bull market that began in 2009 had gone on for so long. He was frustrated with the Fed, which he believed was using financial tools to keep the bull market artificially alive longer than was reasonable. He was convinced there would be a day of reckoning, one that would have disastrous consequences.

The following is an interview I did with Mark about bear markets.

Can you predict a bear market?

Cook: Many people try to predict the next bear market, and most are wrong. Trying to predict the beginning or end of a bear market is impossible. Instead of playing this parlor game, your time should be spent creating a plan for when it does arrive. Preparation is the key to surviving a bear market.

What should someone do if there is a bear market?

Cook: A long-lasting bear market is a tricky animal. At some point, the bear will offer a buying opportunity. Until then, follow your plan, which should include owning a diversified portfolio, plenty of cash on hand for emergencies and buying opportunities, and stocks or index funds for the long term.

It's also important to be emotionally prepared for a bear market. Bear markets are the most painful for investors who borrowed stocks on margin. It's bad enough to lose the money that you invested, but it's much worse when you lose money and must repay. That increases the pain by double.

What is a bear trap?

Cook: There are times when the market is sinking, perhaps near the end of a bear market, and short sellers and others continue to pile in on the short side. Instead of sinking further, the market stalls and then reverses direction. That tricks the bears into shorting even more heavily, and they get smashed on the rally. It's a trap.

Should investors dollar-cost-average on the way down?

Cook: This is a controversial question. There are many professionals who advise that no matter how the market is performing, you should stick to the dollar-cost-averaging strategy of adding a set amount of money for a set time period, such as every month. With this strategy, you get to buy more stocks at lower and lower prices. The expectation and hope is that the bear market will end one day, and that the indexes will reverse direction.

If that happens, all the shares you bought as the market was falling will turn into nice gains. There is no guarantee that the indexes will recover anytime soon, but the odds are good those investments will turn into winners.

Critics say that you are investing good money after bad money. They say that you shouldn't be adding to a losing stock position. There is no guarantee the stock you bought by dollar-cost averaging will recover.

The worst-case scenario, which is rare, occurs when we enter a long-term bear market. Then as you keep buying at lower and lower prices, the market continues to move lower until it becomes a landslide.

What happens in a crash?

Cook: A crash is typically a frightening but short-lived event that brings the market to ridiculously low levels within a few days or weeks. They are destructive and short-lived. One of the worst crashes in history occurred in 2008 when the S&P 500 made a satanic low of 666. It destroyed lives, confidence, and companies.

At first, people believe it is a buying opportunity, but as the market falls faster and farther, it becomes a deadly force. As it accelerates to the downside, it becomes an avalanche.

Even buy-the-dippers lose money as the market goes down farther and faster than anyone predicted. Buy and hold investors are told to sit tight as they watch their money go down the drain. Many people are afraid to sell early because they are afraid of missing out on the next rally.

Are there clues of a crash?

Cook: No one knows the reason for a crash. There are only hints but no smoking gun. It's only in hindsight that you can see the clues. Not surprisingly, before a crash, many people believe that the market is invincible, and that it never will go down. That's when crashes occur, when investors are caught off guard thinking the market has nowhere to go but up.

For example, during the 1987 and 2008 crashes, the market was rising on nothing but fumes. Eventually it just couldn't go any higher and ran out of gas—and reversed. It remains a mystery how a market turns from an ugly sell-off into a major sell-off.

The higher the market goes, the higher the probability that there will be a huge decline. The market will fall harder than anyone can imagine. At the top, no one thinks the market will go down.

What do you look for when the market is collapsing?

Cook: I look for the speed of the movement, which increases volume, volatility, and, therefore, opportunity. You can make more money in bear markets because the market goes down three times faster than it goes up in a bull market. It goes down quicker and is more liquid. A collapse creates speed, frenzy, panic, and chaos.

What happens after a crash?

Cook: Many people believe that a buying opportunity arrives right after a crash, but this is not usually true. Any rallies after a crash are weak, at least at first. Most people prefer to see a correction rather than a crash because the internals of the market remain intact. With a crash, everything gets out of whack, and it's hard for people to regain enough confidence to buy stocks anytime soon.

The smartest thing to do after a crash is to be patient. It's possible the crash will turn into a bear market. People are afraid to risk their retirement money by investing in the market, so buying is tepid or nonexistent.

The stock market can be in the dead zone for years after a bear market. It can take a long time for portfolios to heal, if ever. Typically, the longer a bull market continues, the longer the bear market.

What causes a bear market?

Cook: No one knows. It can come out of nowhere. Often there are clues before it occurs, and sometimes it just happens quickly when the indexes plunge and take all of your profits with it.

What should investors do in a bear market?

Cook: One thing that must be stressed is that bear markets are not always bad. Think of corrections and bear markets as trading opportunities. There is a pause in buying and then an all-out run for the hills when the grizzly is on their heels. When a bear market arrives, people descend into irrational thinking and actions. It *always* happens.

Take the opportunity to learn about down trending markets. You should also prepare for the next bull market that will emerge once the bear market ends. That's when you can really do well. While trading on the short side involves good timing skills and experience, it's easier to trade in a rising market.

Any final thoughts?

Cook: If you buy what no one wants and sell what everyone wants, you will never go bankrupt. I ponder these words daily. That simple approach has guided me throughout my career, but it took me years to understand it. I also learned that the more people who have the same opinion, the greater the probability that the opinion is wrong. During the next bear market, a Pandora's box of horrors will be released. I say this not to create a panic, but to save financial lives.

THE SHORTING TACTICS OF JESSE LIVERMORE

Anyone who has read any of my previous books knows I've learned a lot from Jesse Livermore, considered one of the greatest stock pickers in history. A brilliant but imperfect man, the ups and downs of his life resembled a Greek tragedy.

Livermore became famous when he successfully shorted the stock market during the 1929 crash, earning more than $100 million in a single week. It was his greatest achievement, but it ended in heartbreak and tragedy.

He left home at 14 years of age to find a job at the brokerage firm Paine Webber in Boston. The owners were so impressed by Livermore's ability to solve complex mathematical calculations in his head that he was hired immediately. It didn't hurt that Livermore had a photographic memory.

After watching how stocks acted when they reached certain prices, Livermore made his first stock trade when he was 15 years old, earning a fast $5 profit (a decent amount of money in 1892). He also observed how the firm's most successful customers made money. It didn't take long for Livermore to get hooked on the stock market. He recorded the lessons he learned in his notebook, a ritual he repeated for the rest of his life.

Years later, Livermore used the detailed notes of his trades to publish a book about the experiences of Larry Livingston, a thinly disguised biography. The book, *Reminiscences of a Stock Operator* by Edwin Lefèvre, became a bestseller and is still in demand today. Many of the lessons that Livermore discovered, including trend trading, were way ahead of their time, and quite controversial.

By the time Livermore was 20 years old, he had made so much money that he quit working to become a full-time stock speculator. He started trading stocks in unregulated "bucket shops," unlicensed brokerages that were more like gambling dens than brokerage firms. At bucket shops, customers made directional bets that were booked by the shop itself rather than invested in the market.

Livermore was so successful at guessing market direction that he was banned from every bucket shop in Boston, and then in the United States. Bucket shop owners were always on the lookout for the trader they nicknamed "The Boy Plunger." Livermore often had to wear disguises to try to sneak into a bucket shop to trade for even one day.

He got his nickname because of his youthful looks, and also because of his strategies: When he was sure he was right, he would "plunge" into a position with all his money, earning huge sums when he guessed correctly; but in the process, he damaged the accounts of the bucket shops.

Livermore stopped going to bucket shops after his life was threatened by one unsavory owner, who was not used to losing money to customers. In a way, it was a blessing in disguise; Livermore began trading at traditional brokerage firms, although he did have to adjust his strategies. He went from trading at the bucket shops to trading on the Big Board, the nickname for the New York Stock Exchange (NYSE).

An Imperfect but Brilliant Trader

Although Livermore was a gifted trader, he made many mistakes. Perhaps one of the biggest was that he unknowingly crossed over from trading into gambling. This was one of the reasons he went bankrupt three times. It was his plunging strategy, and a failure to follow his own rules, that caused him the most grief.

Fortunately, each time that Livermore went bankrupt, brokerage firms with which he did business gladly gave him startup money, knowing that with his trading skills, he'd eventually recover the lost cash.

Livermore learned from his experiences that short-term trading was very unpredictable. On some days, he was wildly successful. For example, one time he turned $10,000 into $50,000 within days by betting on only one stock. Then days later, he'd lose all the gains he had just made. He often shorted stocks, which was not a popular strategy at the time.

Eventually, Livermore transformed from a day trading scalper betting on small stock fluctuations into a longer-term trend trader.

It took years of study, but Livermore eventually learned to wait for clues that told him when to buy or sell. Sometimes the clues were hunches, and other times they were based on information that he had heard. He spent much of his time studying stock prices, which became the basis of his trading strategies.

Livermore's Trading Methods

Livermore also learned that it was important to observe the overall stock market because it also gave clues to market direction. In fact, he said that studying general market conditions was one of his greatest discoveries. In addition, instead of predicting what the market was going to do next, his former strategy, he began to look for signals that helped him decide when to buy or sell.

Livermore eventually created a "rules-based" trading system. He often said that when he followed his rules, he made money. When he didn't follow his rules, he lost money.

He made other discoveries. Livermore began to use a strategy called *pyramiding*, a tactic that involved adding to positions as they advanced in price. The idea of buying more shares of stock when your bet is winning compounds your returns.

If the stock continued to rally, and if Livermore was correct, he could substantially increase his profits. A further price increase confirmed that he was right. The compounding effect increased profits, leading to frequent huge gains.

Buy at New Highs

Livermore also bought stocks after they had made a new high, a method later used by many successful investors and traders such as Nicolas Darvas and William O'Neil.

One of Livermore's best ideas was to "probe" before he made an investment. Previously, he used to purchase 1,000 shares of a stock at one time. Sometimes he was right and made money, but when he was wrong, the losses were disappointing. With the probe, he would begin by buying only 200 shares, and if proved right, he would keep adding 200 shares, until he owned the full 1,000 shares.

Basically, he bought small positions at the beginning of a trade to test whether the stock was moving in the right direction. If the initial probe was successful, he would add more shares to his winning trades: buying more shares as they rallied further, and shorting more shares as they continued to decline.

How Livermore Made Millions

Livermore continued to use pyramiding and probing strategies, and they worked. On October 24, 1907, using his methods, Livermore made $3 million in a single day shorting the market as it plunged.

The only reason he stopped shorting was that the most famous banker in America, J. P. Morgan, personally asked him to stop to prevent a financial collapse. Livermore told others that he felt like a "King for the day." It was his finest hour, and his reputation grew along with his bank account.

Eventually, Livermore developed a strategy where he looked for "big swings" in the market. He discovered that if he could find market leaders, the stocks that participated in strong uptrends, he could make substantial profits, and he did. He joined in the bull market of the 1920s, profiting handsomely along with everyone else.

Shorting the 1929 Bull Market

However, in late 1928, Livermore began to believe that the market was overextended. As most people know, the market had been rising at a phenomenal pace for a decade. As the market began to move sideways during the summer of 1929, Livermore put out probes on the short side. He paid attention when his probes began to work, even though many of them were costly.

There were many signs that trouble was brewing in the stock market. First, the leading stocks at that time had stopped making new highs, which turned out to be a red flag, although few knew it at that time.

In addition, wise traders like Bernard Baruch and Joseph Kennedy were quietly selling their positions as the market continued to rally. In retrospect, the market was so overbought, there weren't enough buyers to move the market much higher.

In October 1929, the market crashed. After his probes had worked, Livermore plunged into the market on the short side with margin, making over $100 million in one week. Some people even blamed him for the crash because he was one of the few that had benefited. As most know, millions of investors lost everything in the stock market, and the Great Depression soon followed.

Livermore's Downfall

Even after making a fortune in 1929, Livermore filed for bankruptcy for the third time in 1934, only five years after the greatest payday of his life. While plunging earned him a fortune during the 1929 crash, it was also how he went bankrupt. Plunging is similar to betting it all on red or black at a casino and is the exact opposite of proper risk management.

Losing all his money and suffering other personal problems caused Livermore to become severely depressed. In 1940, while in the middle of a deep depression, he ordered a drink at the bar of his favorite New York restaurant, got up and went into the coatroom, and committed suicide with a handgun.

Although Livermore had once been worth millions, dated glamorous actresses, and once owned a number of large houses and boats, at the time of his death at age 63, his estate was reported to be worth less than $10,000.

NOTE: Portions of this narrative were included in my book, *Make Money Trading Options* (McGraw Hill, 2021).

· · · · · · · ·

Now that you have learned how the pros manage bear markets, it's time to turn the page and discuss selling strategies and tactics. While buying stocks is often more enjoyable, when you don't take the time to learn how to sell, it's easy to lose some or all of your hard-earned gains.

As a special treat, in Part Six I also show you how to sell covered calls, an options strategy that allows you to generate monthly income or cash flow. Even if you are not ready to sell covered calls right now, it is a strategy worth knowing.

PART SIX

SELLING STOCKS AND OPTIONS

B elieve it or not, this is the final part (time really flies!). Throughout this book, you have learned a number of different buy and sell signals using technical analysis. Now I want to wrap it up by discussing various selling strategies and tactics. My hope is that you recognize that selling a position is as important as buying.

I have also included a popular options strategy that will appeal to anyone whose primary objective is buying and holding stocks. This strategy, *selling covered calls*, is for conservative investors who want to "rent" their stocks to option buyers for short time periods. In return for "lending" the stock, you receive compensation—that is, cash.

You may wonder what an options strategy is doing in a stock market book. The reason is simple: This is an excellent money-making strategy for anyone who knows about the stock market (which is now you). There is no rush to learn this strategy, but it's there if you're interested.

Now, let's discuss a number of different stock-selling ideas.

CHAPTER 18

THE ART OF SELLING

Most traders and investors spend a lot of time thinking about which stocks to buy but less time thinking about selling. In reality, selling is not only as important as buying, but in many ways, even more important.

While buying is a pleasant experience because we anticipate making money, and is even more enjoyable when choosing winning stocks, selling at the right time can be challenging. It seems that no matter when a stock is sold, you never get the highest price. That is frustrating for a lot of traders.

If you sell too early, even with gains, it's annoying to watch a stock run higher, thinking you missed out on profits. If you sell too late, it's infuriating to watch a winner turn into a loser.

In fact, nothing is more painful to your ego and account than losing all your previous gains. Some investors solve this problem by adopting a "never sell" attitude. While this idea works during bull markets, it can lead to major losses during a correction or bear market.

In the end, it's a personal choice if and when to sell. Because you are reading this book, I assume that you prefer to use indicators and oscillators to guide your exit decision. That's a wise choice.

I also offer a few ideas that may be useful. Some of these ideas you may find meaningful and others you may not. Choose the ones that make the most sense to you and ignore the rest.

SELLING STOCKS

As you know, there are two main reasons for selling stocks or any other security. First, sell to lock in gains. Second, sell to avoid losses. With that in mind, let's explore a number of selling strategies and tactics.

Three Basic Selling Guidelines

Here are three of the most basic selling guidelines that everyone should consider:

1. **Use limit orders, not market orders.** With a limit order, you control the price, but not always the timing. With a market order, you control the timing, but it may not get filled at a price that is good for you. That's why limit orders are usually the better choice even when it takes more time to work the order.

    On the other side of this issue, using a limit order can result in missing the sale altogether. That happens when the stock price changes just as your order is entered.

2. **Never use market orders in the premarket.** And I mean *never*. Fortunately, some brokers block market orders in the premarket, and that's a good thing. Leave after-hours trading to the pros.

3. **Don't be in a rush to sell a stock.** Rarely is it necessary to sell a stock "right now." The only exception occurs when you must cut losses immediately or lock in gains during a fast-moving market. Typically, the rush of adrenaline that you feel leads to bad decisions.

Now I'll introduce two important selling ideas.

Idea #1: Sell Losers Quickly

The number one rule for managing risk is to sell losers quickly. Each trader has a different definition for "loser" and "quickly." For example, a *day trader* may sell a losing stock within minutes. On the other hand, *swing* or *position traders* may sell a week or month later, depending on their profit-loss objective. No matter when you sell, the goal is to exit a losing trade in a timely manner.

In addition, you can define *loser* as any stock position that is underwater. For me, a loser is a position that has lost a predefined percentage. For example, you could cut your losses if the stock price declined by 3 to 5 percent. Others may cut losses at 7 or 8 percent. There is no right answer because it depends on your goals for the stock.

It's not easy to cut losers. Traders enter the trade with high hopes, so when the stock price goes in the wrong direction, it's difficult for some traders to admit they were wrong.

Many believe that if they hold on a little longer, the losing stock will come back to even or make a miraculous recovery. In the real world, losing stocks tend to keep losing. And yet many traders just can't let go of their darlings (remember when David and his friends fell in love with Athenex?).

If it helps you to remember, put a sign on your wall or computer that says "Sell Losers." Sometimes a losing stock turns into a winner, but not often enough to ignore these rules. If someone has a better selling strategy, please let me know. Until then, sell those losers!

Idea #2: Set a Stop-Loss Price or Percentage

This is one of the most basic selling ideas but also one of the most important. Before buying a stock, know in advance where to exit the trade. After you make the purchase, enter the stop-loss order. Each trader can determine their own stop-loss price or percentage.

As mentioned earlier, a reasonable strategy is limiting losses to no more than 7 to 8 percent. Each trade is different, so be flexible with the selling decision.

You can create a mental or hard stop loss (which we'll discuss in the sidebar at the end of this chapter), but the main rule is simple: Set your own specific percentage or dollar amount. That prevents a small loss from turning into a big loss.

When a stock is sinking, it isn't the time to hope or wish. Ask yourself: Why am I holding this stock at its current price? Cut the loss at your predefined point and deploy the money elsewhere.

THE BOTTOM LINE: Following this one rule prevents severe losses. The problem is that our emotions, usually hope, prevent us from selling when our stop-loss price is reached.

SOMETIMES YOU HAVE TO BREAK THE RULES

One of the reasons that trading is as much art as science is the exceptions. You just read about quickly selling losers at a predetermined price. And yet there are times, especially at the market open, when that may be the wrong move.

For example, one morning you wake up and find that your stock gapped lower by 10 percent in the premarket. Perhaps the company missed estimates or there was breaking bad news. By the time the market opens, your stock is lower by 12 percent or more. I've seen this happen dozens of times with some of the best companies in the world.

When the stock price of a strong company takes a hit, don't panic. It's possible the decline is temporary, so in this scenario it may be wise to wait. This is one of those times when you may have to ignore the "cut your loss" rule.

The odds are good that the stock price of excellent companies will recover most, if not all, of its losses. A lot depends on the reason for the sell-off; sometimes it takes a long time for the stocks to recover.

If you're feeling panicky, that is the wrong time to sell. However, it's the right time to look at the plan you created to help you through these setbacks. You do have an emergency selling plan, right? If not, it's time to create one with specific instructions of what to do when disaster strikes.

> **THE BOTTOM LINE:** Most of the time, stopping the financial bleeding and cutting losses is the correct decision. On occasion, it's appropriate to wait a while longer, maybe even a few more days, to see how the stock reacts.

After reading this, I hope that you think about when to sell as much as when to buy. The next idea should help get you started.

HAVE A SELLING PLAN

A selling or trade plan is a list of "what to do" rules. If you don't have a plan, especially during volatile markets, you are playing it by ear, and that often leads to random trade results. A plan or script, similar to a road map, helps traders make good decisions in times of emotional stress.

It's a good idea to have a profit-taking plan as well as an escape plan for losing trades. Before buying any stock, consider in advance at what price you will plan to cut losses or lock in gains.

Use the numerous sell signals mentioned in the technical analysis chapters. Or perhaps your analysis tells you that a 20 percent profit is all that you can expect. In that case, set that as the target and enter a sell order near that price.

You have many choices. The main point is to have a solid selling strategy ready to implement as soon as you press the Enter key and buy the shares.

HINT: Use your brokerage software to set up alerts, including sell triggers when certain price points are reached. Automating a hard stop removes the decision process and forces the financial product to be sold.

Unfortunately, the stock market does not offer "mulligans" (do-overs). If you make a mistake or lose money, no matter the reason, that money is gone. After selling a position, don't dwell on how much money "you could have made" if you hadn't sold.

Your only choice is to learn from your mistakes and do better the next time. The faster you can accept losses as part of doing business as a trader, the better. Use that pain to become a more informed trader, investor, and person.

Some traders are unable to accept defeat and seek revenge on a stock. Don't fall for that emotional trap. If you lose money, let it go and move on to another trade. There are many fish in the stock market sea.

Now that I have you thinking, let's discuss a number of specific selling tactics that may help manage positions.

Tactic #1: Scale Out of a Position When a Stock Is Overbought

It's not easy to sell when your stock keeps moving higher. If gains are good, it may be wise to scale out of the position in quarters or halves. The main point is to think about taking something off the table. Sure, you will miss further gains if the stock keeps rising. However, the alternative is the possibility of watching a decent gain disappear. Unfortunately, no one can predict which stocks will continue rising and which will reverse.

As the saying goes, "It's better to be safe than sorry." Discipline means ignoring feelings of greed and selling at least a portion of the position when a stock or index gets extremely overbought.

You previously read about scaling *into* a position when buying. It's the same procedure when scaling *out* of a position. For example, if you own 1,000 shares, sell 250 shares at a time. If you have reasons to sell more, perhaps 500 shares, then do so. This strategic selling method is better than lump-sum selling in a panic.

In the old days, this strategy would have been commission-costly, but no longer. You can scale out of a position with as many or as few shares as you wish, and for no cost as nearly all brokerage firms are commission-free.

Tactic #2: Sell Half (or All)

This strategy is similar to scaling out of a position but in fewer steps. Begin by selling half the position; then sell the other half. Perhaps the stock is dropping quickly and you want to cut your losses quickly. Or perhaps the stock price gapped at the open and you want to lock in some profit and let the other half run higher. In both examples, selling half is a good strategy.

> **NOTE:** I found that selling the entire position often works best with losers. With winners, however, it's often wise to sell only half and hold the rest. The theory is that winners keep winning while losers keep losing.
>
> Remember this important quote by the financier and trader Bernard Baruch: "Repeatedly in my market operations I have sold a stock while it still was rising—and that has been one reason why I have held onto my fortune."

Tactic #3: Sell Quickly When You Make a Mistake

It's annoying when a brand-new position begins to lose money immediately. Perhaps you entered at an unlucky time or received a poor execution on your order. Losses could be immediate, and there is nothing to be done about that. But this does not mean that you made a mistake.

Sometimes markets go against your indicators. That's part of trading. You must realize that these indicators do not work 100 percent of the time. Therefore, don't always blame yourself when a trade loses money. Your job now is to manage the trade.

If the indicators still issue a "go long" signal, then stay with the trade. On the other hand, some trades must be tagged as losers, and when that happens, don't hesitate to sell, even when it's on the same day you made your purchase. Some readers may consider this day trading, and perhaps it is, but it's better to cut losses quickly than be stuck with a position that does not belong in your portfolio.

> **THE BOTTOM LINE:** There's nothing wrong with getting out of a bad trade quickly. It's a necessary part of trading. Then try again another day.

Tactic #4: Move Some of Your Profits into Less Risky Products

You have already read how Jesse Livermore made over $100 million in a week during the 1929 stock market crash. He continued to speculate using risky strategies such as doubling down and plunging. As a result, he lost all his money within five years. One of his biggest regrets was not moving some of his gains into cash or fixed-income securities.

This also happened to one of my elderly neighbors. He was sitting on a gain of over $800,000 in one stock. Instead of selling shares so he could pay off his mortgage or put some aside for emergencies, he held on for dear life.

When his stock collapsed during a bear market, he lost most of his money, and also his house because he could no longer afford his mortgage payments. I had warned him that he had too much money in one stock, but he dismissed my concerns: "I know what I am doing."

Here's a suggestion: Learn from the mistakes of others, including my neighbor. Routinely take *some* profits off the table just in case there is a worst-case scenario. It doesn't mean selling all just because you have huge profits. But think about selling some of the position and moving those earnings to a safer place.

Tactic #5: Sell Early

Some of the most successful investors in history claim they sell early. Contrarian stock investor Nathan Rothschild, when asked the secret of his success, responded, "I never buy at the bottom, and I always sell too soon."

In addition, investor Bernard Baruch, when asked how he became wealthy, quipped, "I made my money by selling too soon."

Although selling early goes against nearly everything taught in investment classes, following this rule helps to reduce the role of emotions in your trading, especially fear and greed. Granted, it is not easy to sell early, especially with large profits, but no one knows that it's early at the time the trade is made.

Instead of trying to squeeze every last penny from a transaction, the idea is to sell at a price point that brings a decent amount of profits. This strategy also reduces market risk. Rothschild's rule: You must be willing to give up potential gains to reduce risk.

These ideas and guidelines are not meant to be the final word. The more you trade, the more you will learn about when to sell for a satisfactory profit. Unfortunately, there is never a "best" time because we always think we could have done better.

STOP-LOSS ORDERS AND TIME STOPS

In this sidebar, I review two methods for selling stock or other securities. One is the traditional stop loss, and the other is a method you may not have heard about (unless you happen to have read my other books).

Stop-Loss Orders: Protection from Disaster

There are many ways to protect the value of your portfolio in case one or more of your stocks goes in the wrong direction. Some traders use "mental" stop-loss orders; that is, they think of a target price (in their head) and sell when the target is hit. Others may set up an alert system so they are notified when the target is reached.

Both methods are excellent, as long as you don't ignore the alerts, something that is all too common. Therefore, a "hard" stop loss order is a better choice. That is an order to sell a position when the stock price trades at or below a specific level. Set a specific sum, or a percentage of the total amount invested (perhaps 7 percent of the stock price), that you are willing to lose on the trade.

Once a purchase is made and the stop loss is in place, if the stop-loss order is triggered, one of two things will happen: If the order is a stop-loss *market* order, the sale is triggered automatically at the best available price. If the order is a stop-loss *limit* order, the order will become live, but it may not be filled.

I can't stress enough how important it is to think about establishing a sell price as soon as you buy stock. It can be a hard or mental stop-loss order, but decide on an exit point.

THE BOTTOM LINE: Whenever you own a position, establish an exit price as part of your trading plan, and do not leave home without one.

ALERT: During a volatile market, when a stock gaps down, the next available market price could be many points lower than the most recent price. This is one of the problems with hard stop losses.

Time Stops: Sell Based on the Calendar

A *time stop* is a useful but underutilized tactic to cut losses or lock in gains. After buying stock, set a time at which you will sell the position, regardless of whether it is profitable. For example, after buying 100 shares of stock, determine what day or time you plan to sell.

This decision depends on your trading strategy. Obviously, day traders will set an intraday time stop, while long-term traders may use a week, month, or longer. For example, you can sell by Friday (what I call being a *weekly trader*).

· · · · · · · · ·

Now that you have a better understanding of when to sell, in the next chapter, you'll learn how to sell covered calls. It is a conservative options strategy that brings income or cash flow. I have included it for anyone who wants to use stocks they own to generate extra income.

CHAPTER 19

SELLING COVERED CALL OPTIONS

Y ou may be wondering what a chapter on selling options is doing in a book on the stock market. The reason this strategy is in the book is simple: After you have learned all about the stock market, there may come a time when you want to generate extra income or cash flow by "renting" stocks that you own to others.

For that reason, I decided to include this conservative options strategy, selling covered calls, in this book. (Another reason was that I wrote a bestselling book, *Understanding Options*, and wanted to introduce one of the best strategies in the book.)

If you have your hands full learning about the stock market and have no desire to learn about options, feel free to skip this chapter. It will be here if you decide to use it in the future. On the other hand, if the idea of selling options on stocks you own sounds intriguing, then continue reading. You are about to enter a different world using completely new vocabulary.

NOTE: This is the shortened, introductory version of selling covered calls.

WHY YOU SHOULD TRADE OPTIONS

If you heard that options are too risky or are only for speculators, I have a surprise for you. Although there are many options strategies that are speculative, the strategy I'll introduce in this chapter is for investors. I believe you will enjoy reading about this strategy—selling options is like having your cake and eating it, too.

Here are the four main reasons why anyone would buy or sell options:

- Increase income
- Protect a stock portfolio
- Hedge against stock market risk
- Speculate

In this chapter I show how to increase income by *selling covered calls*. With the covered call strategy, you sell options on stocks that you already own, thereby generating income or cash flow.

SELLING COVERED CALLS

There are two main reasons for selling covered calls (also known as *writing covered calls*):

1. To bring in income or increase cash flow on stocks you already own
2. To sell stocks that you no longer want in your portfolio

With this strategy, you "rent" your stock to the option buyer. In return, the buyer must pay a fee (called a *premium*) for the right to buy your shares of stock at a predetermined price (the *strike price*). The premium is the money received for giving up control of your stock.

NOTE: The specialized terms included in the above paragraph will be thoroughly explained in this chapter.

The risk of selling covered calls is that the price of your underlying stock falls by more than the premium collected. Even with this risk, if you are new to the options market, selling covered calls is one of the first strategies you should try.

LEARN OPTIONS VOCABULARY

In many ways, learning about options is similar to learning a new language. At first, it may seem confusing. However, once you learn the unique vocabulary and make your first trade, it becomes a lot easier.

Here are some facts about options that should help you understand how it works:

- Stock options are contracts that give their owners the right to buy or sell stock. Every stock option is linked or attached to a specific stock, known as the *underlying stock*. One of the terms you'll see used to describe options is *derivative*, meaning the value is derived from another financial instrument. In this example, that instrument is a specific stock.
- There are only two types of options: *calls* and *puts*. Calls allow the owner to buy stock (a bullish strategy), and puts allow the owner to sell stock (a bearish strategy). Although there are dozens of fancy-sounding options strategies, all are based on buying and selling calls and puts.
- In this chapter, we will only discuss *selling* call options. When selling a call option on shares of stock that you own, it is known as a *covered* call.
- When you sell covered calls, the premium is collected up front and is yours to keep. This is the primary reason why

this strategy makes sense for investors, and why it's important to learn.

- There is something else you should know about options: 1 *call option* represents the "right" to buy 100 shares. Therefore, 5 option contracts equal 500 shares. If you own 200 shares, you can sell either 1 or 2 covered call contracts.

- Another unique aspect of options is that they have an *expiration date*. At a date and time specified in the contract, the option expires. Once expiration arrives, either an option is converted into a stock position, or it's worthless (it has no value). When selling options, the passage of time is a positive feature.

  Unlike option buyers, who worry about losing all their money when expiration arrives, option sellers welcome expiration. At expiration, two good things can happen: Either the option expires worthless and option sellers continue to hold their stock (assuming that their strategy is selling covered calls), or their stock is sold at the strike price, locking in the desired profit.

- The *strike price* is the fixed price at which the call owner can buy or the put owner can sell the underlying stock. If this seems confusing, it will make more sense when you study the examples later in this chapter.

- Selling covered calls is considered a conservative options strategy that is less risky than buying calls and puts. That doesn't mean there is no risk, but option sellers typically lose less money than option speculators do.

HOW TO SELL COVERED CALLS

Now that you have a basic understanding of the options vocabulary used by covered call sellers (writers), let's take a closer look at how to sell covered calls. To review, when you sell call options, you receive cash (the premium).

In return, you accept the obligation to sell, for example, 1 call option, or 100 shares of your stock at a certain price (the strike price) for a limited time (until expiration). No matter what happens to the stock price, you get to keep the premium.

If this is your first experience with options, this will become clearer as you keep reading. Be sure that you first understand the concepts before trading, which takes time. The following example should be helpful.

SELLING YOUR FIRST COVERED CALL

On June 17, you own 100 shares of ZYX Corporation, which is currently trading at $34 per share. After signing into your brokerage account, look at the *option chain* (a list of calls and puts that are available for trading with their current *bid-ask price*, *expiration dates*, and *strike prices*).

After studying the option chain, you decide to sell 1 call contract (1 contract = 100 shares) with a July 18 expiration date (one month away). You choose an option with a $35 strike price. That means the call owner has the right to buy your shares at $35 per share. This right expires when the expiration date arrives (the third Friday of the expiration month, or July 18 in this example).

Your only obligation is to sell your stock at $35 per share no matter how high or low the stock goes. Even if the stock price rises to $40, you are obligated to sell your stock at $35, the strike price.

NOTE: You must sell your stock at the strike price only if the option holder decides to *exercise* the option to buy the shares.

If the stock is less than $35 at expiration, then the call owner will not elect to take your shares (exercise the option), and you get to keep the stock as well as the premium you received.

When looking at the bid-ask price for the ZYX July 18 call, you see that the bid price is $2.40 per share. Therefore, expect to collect at least $240 for each call sold.

> **NOTE:** If you own 200 shares, then the premium (the cash you receive) for selling 2 calls is $480. If you own 500 shares, then the premium for selling 5 calls is $1,200.

After selling the call, you must continue owning the underlying stock (in this case, ZYX) until the option expires on July 18. It's a fair trade; in the above example, you were paid a premium ($240) for accepting the obligation to sell those shares at $35.

What could go wrong with the covered call strategy? First, if the price of ZYX declines by more than the premium, you would lose money. The second problem is that you lose out on any gains above the strike price. No matter how high ZYX goes, you are obligated to sell 100 shares of ZYX at $35 per share. If you think you own a winning stock that will rise by a huge amount, selling covered calls is not the right strategy.

The ideal market for a call seller is one in which stocks are going sideways or slightly higher. In a sideways market, certain stocks are unlikely to move very high, which is why selling covered calls is so popular with investors.

> **HINT:** Look for stocks on your Watch List that fit the characteristics of the ideal covered call candidate. A stock that is flat or slightly bullish is a good place to start. The worst environment for selling covered calls is a bear market or a stock that is headed lower.

IF YOU STILL AREN'T SURE HOW TO SELL COVERED CALLS

As a former teacher, I know that it takes time to learn a new strategy such as selling covered calls. I also remember the difficulties that I had when learning it for the first time. That is why I've included additional examples to help you further understand this strategy. That is also why I may repeat some of the information above by using other examples.

> **NOTE:** If you already know how to sell covered calls, feel free to skip the following review.

DIGGING A LITTLE DEEPER

The reason to sell covered calls is to generate income while reducing the risk of owning a stock. When the stock price falls, any loss is reduced by the premium collected. This strategy is also allowed in an IRA or 401(k), but speak to a tax professional before tapping into these accounts. You also must be approved for options trading by your broker before using any options strategy.

As mentioned earlier, there are two potential risks: The first is that the stock price may plunge, always a risk when owning stock. Second, potential gains above the strike price will go to the option owner and not to you.

When you sell a covered call, you must own shares of the underlying stock. Then you sell someone the "right" to buy those shares at a set price (the strike price) until the option expires. The strike price is part of the contract and does not change no matter which way the market goes.

NOTE: When you own the underlying stock, the call is *covered*. If you don't own the underlying stock, it is known as a *naked* or *uncovered* call, a strategy not suitable for option newcomers.

Why would you want to sell the rights to your stock? Because you receive cash. For some people, receiving extra income on stocks is so desirable that they are willing to give up on the possibility of large gains.

EXAMPLE #1: SELLING A COVERED CALL

Let's say in February you own 100 shares of XYZ, currently $40 per share. You decide to sell one call.

The Strike Price

You, the option seller, agreed to sell those 100 shares at an agreed-upon price, known as the strike price. Looking at the option chain, you find an assortment of strike prices. The strike price of the option you choose determines how much premium is collected when selling the option. For call options, as the strike price increases, the premium decreases.

This means that an option with a $35 strike price is always more expensive than one with a $37 strike price. Why? The right to pay $35 per share is worth more than the right to pay $37 per share. The bottom line is the lower the strike price, the more it costs to purchase a call option.

The Expiration Date

In addition to deciding on the most appropriate strike price, you also choose an expiration date, the third Friday of the expiration month. Let's say in February you choose a May expiration date. On the third Friday in May, trading on the option ends.

At the expiration date, there are two main choices: Either your option is *assigned* (forcing the stock sale at the strike price), or you keep the stock. Because some people don't want to tie up their stock for too long, they may choose expiration dates that are only a month or two away.

> **HINT:** The further the expiration date, the more valuable the option, because additional time gives the underlying stock more opportunity to move far past the strike price.

> **NOTE:** Experience helps investors find strike prices and expiration dates that suit their risk-reward profiles. As a new option investor, carefully consider the price at which you are willing to unload your stock and how much premium is needed to generate a return that is acceptable to you.

EXAMPLE #2: SELLING A COVERED CALL

It's January 15, and you own 100 shares of ZYX, currently at $50 per share. You decide to sell one covered call with a $52 strike price that expires on February 20. The *bid* price for this option is $1.25.

If you were willing to initiate this trade over the phone, you'd say to the broker, "I'd like to sell one ZYX February 52 call at a limit price of $1.25 good for the day only. It's covered."

If the call sells at $1.25, as you expect, the premium received is $125 (100 shares × $1.25).

> **HINT:** Always place a limit order, not a market order.

Let's take a look at what could go right, or wrong, with this transaction.

- **SCENARIO ONE.** The underlying stock, ZYX, is *above* the $52 strike price on the expiration date.

    If the underlying stock is above the strike price at expiration, even by one penny, the stock will be "called away." In options terminology, this means the stock is taken out of your account and sold at the strike price. To fulfill the terms of the option contract, you are obligated to sell 100 shares at $52 (in this example). The trade occurs on February 20.

    Some people sell covered calls month after month to generate cash flow. If you adopt the covered call strategy, you must plan for and expect to sell your shares at least part of the time. If your stock is called away, you can always repurchase the shares and sell another covered call.

    One of the criticisms of selling covered calls is that it limits gains. In other words, if ZYX suddenly zoomed to $57 per share, the stock would still be sold at $52 (the strike price). You would not participate in the gains past the strike price. If you are looking to make a big score, then selling covered calls is not an ideal strategy.

    - **Benefit.** You keep the premium, any stock gains up to the strike price, and dividends.
    - **Risk.** You forfeit potential gains above the strike price. In addition, your stock is tied up—you cannot sell it until the expiration date.

NOTE: If the stock is less than $48.75 (the current stock price minus premium) at expiration, then you lost money on the position. However, the $125 premium received still provides a better outcome than that of every other shareholder who did not sell a covered call.

- **SCENARIO TWO.** The underlying stock is *below* the strike price on the expiration date.

    If the underlying stock is below $52 (strike price) at the close of business on expiration day, the option has expired unexercised and is now worthless. You keep the stock and the premium. As mentioned earlier, you can always sell another covered call if you wish.

    Although some people hope their stock price declines so they can keep both the shares and the premium, be careful what you wish for. For example, if ZYX declines to $45 per share, the $125 premium reduces the pain, but you still lose $375 (a $500 loss offset by the $125 premium).
    - **Benefit.** The main benefit is that you keep the premium. If the stock is above $48.75, the position has been profitable.
    - **Risk.** You lose money when the stock falls below the $48.75 breakeven price.

- **SCENARIO THREE.** The underlying stock is *near* the strike price on the expiration date.

    Some might say this is the most satisfactory result for a covered call seller. If the underlying stock is slightly below the strike price at expiration, you keep the premium and the stock. You can then sell a covered call for the following month, or any expiration month, bringing in additional income.
    - **Benefit.** You keep the stock and premium and can continue to sell calls on the same stock.
    - **Risk.** The stock falls by more than the collected premium, costing you money.

NOTE: Some people sell covered calls on stocks they no longer want to own. If the strategy is successful, the stock is called away at the strike price. You keep the premium and get to sell the unwanted shares.

IF YOU WANT TO SELL COVERED CALLS

It may be worth your time to learn how to sell covered calls one day. After you thoroughly understand how to make a profit in the stock market, consider learning how to sell covered calls on some of your stocks.

As with any other investment, this is an ideal strategy as long as you choose the "right" stock and the overall market environment is favorable (slightly bullish or flat). For many investors, it's wonderful to receive cash by selling calls on their stocks. It is a strategy that is definitely worth considering.

· · · · · · · · ·

Believe it or not, we have reached the end of the book! In the next section, I wrap up the book with ideas of what you may want to do next. The next part also includes resources for further study and an Indicator Glossary with definitions of all of the most important indicators and oscillators.

WHAT YOU CAN DO NOW

Congratulations for finishing this entire book! I want to thank you for taking the time to read about the many stock market strategies and tactics. I hope that you learned ways to reduce risk while increasing profits.

The detailed discussion on indicators and oscillators should give you additional insights into how to use technical analysis to gain an edge over other traders. This is the scientific part of trading that is essential to your success as a trader.

I am also glad that you know what to expect in case a correction, crash, or bear market arrives. You are certain to experience one of these events (and perhaps all three). The time to prepare is before there is a worst-case scenario.

A theme running through the entire book is the importance of discipline. That means having a set of rules and guidelines and then following them. No matter how good your trading skills, if you lack discipline, then it will be a struggle to make profits.

One way to improve discipline is to keep a trading diary or journal. Write details about your trades as well as recording any mistakes. Making mistakes is a natural part of the trading business. Your goal, however, is not to repeat those mistakes.

I also want to remind you about the importance of diversification. This means having a variety of financial products including stocks, index funds, gold, bonds, and perhaps digital currencies. It's also essential to have cash on the side to deal with emergencies or to buy stocks that are on sale.

If you don't have the money right now to diversify, there is no rush. Invest or trade in what you can afford, but make it a goal to diversify as your income increases and you build wealth over time.

Don't fall into the trap of being forced to make money fast. Making profits in the stock market takes time. For now, focus on being the best trader or investor that you can, and the rest should fall into place. As I've written before, the key to success in the stock market is finding ways to reduce risk. This means using mental or hard stop losses and not making big bets on questionable investments.

I'm not telling you this because it sounds good. This is based on my own painful experiences and those of others who have lost money because we didn't respect risk. Reducing risk should always be your highest priority. Then you can work on increasing profits.

Too many market participants have a laissez-faire attitude toward profits, and they are shocked when the money disappears one day. Since I don't want that to happen to you, do everything in your power to protect any gains.

SINCERE ADVICE

By now, I'm sure you are eager to get started trading, but first I'd like to share a few ideas. These are only suggestions—to be used or discarded as you see fit. These opinions are based on my own successes and failures in the stock market.

- **Buy an index fund.** One of the easiest ways to get started in the stock market is to buy shares of an index fund. This is advice I give in nearly every book I write because it works. You can be a short-term trader while also having a portion of your

money in an untouchable index fund. Resist the urge to take
money out of that account.

- **Invest in a 401(k) or IRA.** If you work at a company, it probably has a 401(k) plan or stock purchase plan. These tax-
deferred products are a fantastic way to build wealth over
the long term. If you have the chance to join an employer-
sponsored plan, then do so, especially if the employer
matches your contribution.

    If you leave the company, you can keep the account with
your previous employer, convert it into an IRA, or roll it
over to your new employer's 401(k) plan (if available). As
always, speak to a tax advisor or accountant before using
any of these products, as the rules frequently change.

- **Buy individual stocks or ETFs.** Now that you've read this book,
you are ready to buy stocks or ETFs. It's hard to go wrong
with buying stocks in companies that have popular products or services, tons of loyal customers, shrewd managers,
and excellent customer service.

    Owning stocks is an excellent way to build wealth, but
be very picky about the stocks that you buy. In this book
I have given you many ideas about how to find winning
stocks. Now go out and find them.

- **Test before you trade.** As you probably know, I'm a believer in
using a simulated or paper money program to make practice
trades. This is an excellent method of fine-tuning your trading skills while also increasing your knowledge. You can even
use the paper money account to identify winning stocks.

- **Make money.** To profit in the stock market, you need the right
mindset, technical tools, discipline, and good timing skills.
No matter your age, you can achieve success. Although I
hope this book helped you to reach these goals, it's up to
you to use what you learned to make money in the stock
market. I believe you can do it.

IT'S TIME TO SAY GOODBYE

Before I go, I'd like to share with you a letter written by my grandfather, a successful owner of a Chicago stock brokerage firm (a *Wall Street Journal* article with similar advice was attached to the letter). The letter contained the following financial advice setting out goals that I believe are worthy today, although not easy for most people to achieve:

1. Begin by paying off all your debts.
2. After being debt-free, you must not be tempted to blow your money on risky financial ventures.
3. It is hard enough for most people to earn a bare living, including 95 percent who are unable to keep and acquire a fortune. This is not to discourage you but to warn you and give you courage to fight harder to be one of the 5 percent.
4. Always be prepared for the possibility that you may have to support your parents.
5. You want the privilege of helping those who are afflicted and impoverished.
6. The most important measure of success is integrity, hard work, and being right more than 55 percent of the time. This also means diversifying risks so that when you are wrong, it won't break or crimp you.
7. Never cosign promissory notes to help others.
8. Never buy stocks in small corporations to please friends— easy to buy, difficult to sell.
9. Don't be easy when it comes to lending money except in extreme cases (i.e., don't let a worthy friend down).
10. Only hard experience, proven by facts, should impress you and cause you to follow the rules just outlined.

Speaking of experience, I have learned that the best investment you can make is in people. You can't go wrong spending money on an education, a home, a new business, your children, pets, or those who desperately need your help. After all, why make money if you don't use it to improve your life or the lives of others?

Learning this much about the stock market can be overwhelming, so don't worry if you feel that way. That feeling will go away as you gain experience. This book offers a solid introduction to short-term trading and investing, but there is much more to learn.

Good luck investing and trading stocks, and thanks again for reading my book. There is always a winning stock somewhere, and it's your job to find it. It's been a pleasure sharing my knowledge and experiences with you, and I wish that all your financial dreams come true.

If you have comments or questions about my book, feel free to send me an email to msincere@gmail.com. In addition, if you notice any errors, please let me know so I can make corrections in the next edition. Finally, if you have time, feel free to visit my website, www.michaelsincere.com.

RESOURCES

f you want to do additional research, including visiting websites and reading books devoted to the stock market, the following resources should be helpful.

BOOKS

For Beginner Investors

One Up on Wall Street by Peter Lynch and John Rothchild (Simon & Schuster, 2000). How to profit in the market using a long-term investment approach that includes doing basic research before buying a stock.

The Little Book of Common Sense Investing by John Bogle (Wiley, 2017). Bogle discusses the advantages of using index funds and why they should be in every investor's portfolio.

For Beginner Traders

Reminiscences of a Stock Operator by Edwin Lafèvre (Wiley Investment Classics, 2017). Early classic about the trading experiences of Jesse Livermore, a legendary trader from the early twentieth century.

A Beginner's Guide to Short-Term Trading by Toni Turner (Adams Media, 2008). An easy-to-read book for novice short-term traders that includes useful trading tactics and tools.

Trading for a Living by Alexander Elder (Wiley, 2014). How to master the psychological challenges of the market as well as how to use technical indicators.

Market Wizards (Wiley, 2012) and *The New Market Wizards* (Harper Business, 2008) by Jack D. Schwager. Schwager delves into the minds of profitable traders using a question-and-answer interview format.

How I Made $2,000,000 in the Stock Market by Nicolas Darvas (Martino Fine Books, 2018). Classic book about a stock market novice who uses support and resistance along with pyramiding to make a fortune during a bull market.

Jesse Livermore: Boy Plunger by Tom Rubython (Myrtle Press, 2015). Rubython delves into the life and trading tactics of legendary short seller Jesse Livermore.

How to Make Money in Stocks by William O'Neil (McGraw Hill, 2009). An introduction to CAN SLIM, which shows traders how to make money using a rule-based, systematic approach that combines technical and fundamental analysis.

How to Day Trade for a Living by Andrew Aziz (Manjul Publishing House, 2021). The author helps rookie day traders become full-time day traders.

Trading in the Zone by Mark Douglas (Prentice Hall, 2000). A book on how to master the psychological challenges of short-term trading.

For Experienced Investors

The Intelligent Investor by Benjamin Graham (Harper Business, 2006). Classic book for value investors on how to use fundamental analysis to determine whether a company and its stock is a good investment.

For Experienced Traders

Technical Analysis of Stock Trends by Robert D. Edwards and John Magee (Martino Fine Books, 2011). This classic book introduces traders to all aspects of technical analysis including indicators and oscillators and chart patterns.

Technical Analysis of the Financial Markets by John Murphy (New York Institute of Finance, 1999). Murphy explains all aspects of technical analysis with the help of over 400 charts.

Japanese Candlestick Charting Techniques by Steve Nison (Prentice Hall, 2001). Nison, credited with introducing candlesticks to the West, explains how to trade using candlestick charts.

A Beginner's Guide to High-Risk, High-Reward Investing by Robert Ross (Adams Media, 2022). Ross introduces a number of speculative investment ideas, giving step-by-step instructions for each strategy while backing it up with his personal stories.

INVESTMENT CLUBS AND ASSOCIATIONS

If you want to join an investment club or start your own club, the not-for-profit National Association of Investment Clubs (NAIC) should meet your needs. For membership information, visit the NAIC website at BetterInvesting.org.

USEFUL WEBSITES FOR INVESTORS AND TRADERS

AAII*: http://www.aaii.com

Bankrate: http://bankrate.com

Barchart: http://www.barchart.com

Barron's*: http://www.barrons.com

Benzinga: http://www.benzinga.com

Bloomberg: http://www.bloomberg.com

Briefing: http://www.briefing.com

CNBC: http://www.cnbc.com

CNN Business: http://Money.cnn.com

ETF.com: http://www.etf.com

Financial Times*: http://www.ft.com

Finscreener: http://www.finscreener.com

Finviz: http://www.finviz.com

Forbes magazine: http://www.forbes.com

Fox Business News: http://www.foxbusiness.com

Google Finance: http://www.google.com/finance

Investopedia: http://www.investopedia.com

Investor's Business Daily*: http://www.investors.com

Kiplinger*: http://www.kiplinger.com

Market Chameleon: http://www.marketchameleon.com

MarketWatch: http://www.marketwatch.com

The MoneyShow: http://www.moneyshow.com

Morningstar: http://www.morningstar.com

---

* Indicates paid subscription required.

The Motley Fool: http://www.fool.com

MSN Money: http://www.msn.com

MutualFunds: http://mutualfunds.com

Nasdaq: http://www.nasdaq.com

NerdWallet: http://nerdwallet.com

New York Stock Exchange: http://www.nyse.com

Real Clear Markets: http://www.realclearmarkets.com

SEC: http://www.sec.gov

Seeking Alpha: http://www.seekingalpha.com

Stock Rover*: http://www.stockrover.com

StockCharts: http://www.stockcharts.com

The Street*: http://www.thestreet.com

TradingView: http://www.tradingview.com

Value Line*: http://www.valueline.com

Wall Street Journal: http://www.wsj.com

Yahoo Finance: Finance.yahoo.com

Zacks Investment Research*: http://www.zacks.com

INDICATOR GLOSSARY

Although there are hundreds of technical indicators, the following is a brief list and definitions of the most common indicators found on many brokerage firms' software.

Accumulation Distribution Line (ADL). The ADL is a cumulative indicator that evaluates how much money is flowing into and out of a stock.

Average Directional Index (ADX). The ADX determines the strength of the current trend.

Average True Range (ATR). The ATR is a simple moving average of the true range (difference between high and low each day) and is one method for measuring the volatility of an individual stock.

Bollinger Band Width. This indicator is one of two indicators (the other is %B) that can be derived from Bollinger Bands.

Bollinger Bands. Bollinger Bands measure volatility expansions and contractions using bands that are set two standard deviations above and below the 20-day moving average.

CBOE Nasdaq Market Volatility (VXN). The VXN measures the volatility of the Nasdaq market using the implied volatility of Nasdaq 100 index option prices.

CBOE Volatility Index (VIX). The VIX measures the volatility of 500 stocks in the S&P 500 index using the implied volatility of S&P 500 stock index options.

Chaikin Money Flow (CMF). This indicator is used to determine whether individual stocks are experiencing accumulation (buying) or distribution (selling) pressure.

Chande Momentum Oscillator. This oscillator determines whether a stock is overbought or oversold.

Commodity Channel Index (CCI). Another oscillator, the CCI is used to determine whether a stock is overbought or oversold, in addition to identifying cyclical turns in commodities.

Exponential Moving Average. A moving average that gives greater weight to the most recent closing prices.

Keltner Channel. An envelope indicator with a fixed band, the Keltner Channel measures stock or commodity movements.

McClellan Oscillator. This is a momentum oscillator of net advances (advances less declines). It gives information about advance/decline (A/D) line statistics and measures the acceleration that occurs in the market breadth numbers.

McClellan Summation Index. This breadth indicator identifies the market's current trend.

Money Flow Index (MFI). This is a momentum indicator that measures the strength of money flowing into and out of a stock, either positive or negative.

Moving Average Convergence Divergence (MACD). This is a momentum indicator that shows the relationship between two moving averages and is used to help determine entries or exits.

Moving Average Envelope. This indicator, surrounded by two other moving averages (the envelope), is designed to identify trend changes.

Negative Volume Index. This index analyzes volume decreases from the previous day.

NYSE TICK. Used primarily by intraday traders, the NYSE TICK monitors short-term overbought or oversold conditions by comparing how many of the latest prices are upticks or downticks.

NYSE TRIN (Arms Index). The Arms Index is a breadth indicator that identifies overbought or oversold conditions.

On Balance Volume (OBV). OBV is a momentum indicator that analyzes volume flow into and out of individual stocks.

Parabolic SAR. This is used to set trailing price stops for short or long positions, depending on the direction of the trend.

Positive Volume Index (PVI). This indicator zeros in on the days when volume has increased from the previous day.

Price/Earnings (P/E) Ratio. The granddaddy of fundamental indicators, the price/earnings ratio helps investors determine which stock is a better value.

Price Oscillator (PO). This momentum oscillator, almost identical to MACD, generates buy and sell signals when moving averages diverge and converge.

Price Rate of Change (ROC). This momentum oscillator acts as an overbought or oversold indicator for individual stocks.

Relative Strength Comparison (RSC). This indicator compares a stock's performance with a specific index to determine its relative strength or weakness.

Relative Strength Index (RSI). A momentum indicator, RSI is used to determine overbought or oversold conditions.

Stochastics. This momentum indicator is used to determine overbought and oversold conditions as well as momentum and trend changes. (The calculations behind stochastics are included at the end of this section.)

Volume-Weighted Average Price (VWAP). The VWAP is a trading benchmark that calculates the average price at which a security has traded in one day, based on both volume and price.

Williams %R. The Williams %R momentum indicator is used to determine overbought and oversold conditions.

> **NOTE:** For further information on any of the above indicators, consult the educational sections of StockCharts, Investopedia, or Barchart, or look on your brokerage firm's website.

HOW THE DAILY STOCHASTIC OSCILLATOR IS CALCULATED

I know that a few of you are fascinated by stochastics and want to look under the hood to see how it was constructed. Although not required reading, the following explains the brilliant calculations behind stochastics.

The stochastic chart is composed of three pieces of information: the %K line, the %D line, and the stock's price range. Don't let the unusual nomenclature throw you. The %K line is just a plot of the stochastic oscillator. The %D line is a simple moving average of the last three data points from the %K line. It is a three-day moving average of the %K line.

The %K line compares the lowest low and the highest high over a given period (14 days) to define a price range. It then displays the last closing price as a percentage of this range.

The stock chart in Figure 7.2 (see Chapter 7) includes a vertical line extending from the high and low stock prices (the range) for each day's trading. The most recent closing price is indicated by a horizontal line.

The daily stochastic oscillator is the number that is plotted on the chart. Connecting those points gives the %K line. The daily data point is calculated using these steps:

1. Subtract the low for the (14-day) period from the current closing price.
2. Divide by the total range (highest high minus the lowest low) for the period.
3. Multiply by 100.

Here is an example:

1. Today, XYZ closed at 87.33.
2. During the past 14 days (including today), the highest price was 91.18 and the lowest was 86.04.
3. The stochastic for that day is $100*(87.33 - 86.04)/(91.18 - 86.04) = 25.10$

Next, make the same calculation for as many days back in time as you want to examine and plot the points on a chart. That is the %K stochastic indicator line.

To create the %D line, take the three most recent stochastics (the points plotted to give the %K line) and plot the average.

Because the %D stochastic line is based on a moving average, the %D line is smoother (it changes more slowly) than the %K line. Therefore, the %K line is referred to as the "faster" line, and the %D line is the "slower" line.

I hope that this information will help you understand why stochastics is a favorite with many traders.

ACKNOWLEDGMENTS

To senior editor Judith Newlin at McGraw Hill for her guidance in making this the best possible book. This book could not have been completed without her superb assistance, as well as that of many others at McGraw Hill.

To Stephen Isaacs, my editor at McGraw Hill, for helping me to create two bestselling books. I'll miss his wise advice and insights.

I also appreciate the excellent efforts of Alison Shurtz for helping to create an error-free book.

Thanks also to Patricia Wallenburg for taking this book to the finish line while making sure the final product was of the highest possible quality.

Thanks to Peter Lynch for speaking with me about the stock market and providing insights into how to be a successful investor.

Also thanks to Dr. Marvin Appel (Gerald Appel's son), president of Signalert Asset Management, for sharing additional insights into MACD.

I want to thank CMT Jeff Bierman ("The Quant Guy"), professor of finance at Loyola University in Chicago, for sharing his in-depth insights and experiences about technical analysis.

I am grateful to author, editor, and option expert Mark Wolfinger, who diligently edited and fact-checked every chapter, especially indicators and oscillators. This book could not have been completed without his help.

Thanks to stock dividend expert Warren Kaplan for helping me understand and profit from his dividend stock investment strategies.

I appreciate that Jonathan Burton at MarketWatch offered me so many writing opportunities.

Also thanks to TikTok celebrity Robert Ross for his insights into cryptocurrencies and other high-risk, high-reward strategies.

I am grateful to option expert Mark D. Cook for sharing his knowledge and extensive experience with bear markets. Sadly, he passed away before the book was completed, but I will always remember his sharp wit and blunt warnings about extremely over-bought markets.

Cheers to the hardworking folks at Moon Thai Restaurant in Florida for providing me excellent service and food while I was writing this book.

I also want to express my gratitude to my artistic young neighbor, Lauren, for sharing so many of her imaginative ideas with me. I genuinely hope that she follows the advice in this book so that one day she has the financial freedom to pursue her own dreams.

Jag vill också tacka mina vänner i Sverige, Norge, Danmark, Frankrike, och Tjeckien för deras fantastiska stöd.

Ich danke den vielen deutschen Lesern die meinen letzten Bestseller, *Keine Angst vor Optionen*, gekauft haben.

También agradezco el apoyo de mis amigos en Bolivia, Nicaragua, Colombia, Brasil, Perú, y El Salvador.

Finally, I want to acknowledge the following friends and acquaintances for their support and encouragement: Alexandra Bengtsson, Angela Bengtsson, Harvey Small, Betsy Kagan, Sanne Mueller, Lucie Stejskalova, Hazel Hall, Edith Augustin, Evrice Cornelius, Giovanna Stephenson, Tine Claes, Karina Benzineb, Michael Puyanic, Anna Ridolfo, Chuck Jaffe, and Bert Silverman.

INDEX

Note: Italic page locators refer to figures and tables.

ABOUT THE AUTHOR

MICHAEL SINCERE interviewed some of the top traders and financial experts in the country to find out the lessons they had learned in the market so that he could help others avoid the mistakes he had made.

He wrote a book about these lessons, followed by more books, including *Understanding Options* (McGraw Hill), *Understanding Stocks* (McGraw Hill), *All About Market Indicators* (McGraw Hill), *Start Day Trading Now* (Adams Media), and *Make Money Trading Options* (McGraw Hill).

Sincere has written numerous columns and magazine articles on investing and trading. He has been interviewed on dozens of national radio programs and has appeared on financial news TV programs such as CNBC and ABC's *World News Now* to talk about his books. In addition to being a freelance writer and author, Sincere writes a column for MarketWatch, "Michael Sincere's Long-Term Trader."

If you have questions or comments, write the author at msincere@gmail.com. You can also visit the author's website and read his blog at www.michaelsincere.com.